This book is dedicated to Dr. R.C. Sproul, founder and chairman of Ligonier Ministries. His teachings have brought me to a quiet state of mind about being, especially Ultimate Being, where philosophies and the Judeo-Christian religions can share a correlated concern for ultimate value that must, of logical necessity, have bearing on all things.

You're Just Smart Enough for Hell

Dan Sakall

authorHOUSE®

AuthorHouse™
1663 Liberty Drive, Suite 200
Bloomington, IN 47403
www.authorhouse.com
Phone: 1-800-839-8640

First published by AuthorHouse   3/3/2008

ISBN: 978-1-4343-5079-4 (sc)

Library of Congress Control Number: 2007908706

Printed in the United States of America
Bloomington, Indiana

This book is printed on acid-free paper.

ACKNOWLEDGMENT

This book is number five for me and follows three books in dialogue with God, the Holy Spirit, and Christ. They were received as deeply devotional books. Not long ago, my co-worker and typist, Carol Gulley, asked me a pointed and piercing question: "We have written three books for Christian believers, but not a single one for unbelievers. Why can't you write a book for unbelievers?"

The question stung my conscience. My love is pastoral care in hospitals, where so few unbelievers experience a world view from the mattress. I am not an evangelist at heart. My defense was that I am a BASF company man. This company advertises that they do not make original products, they make them better. I was often heard saying I do not make Christians believers, I labor to make them better. Both Carol and I know right well Who is the real Creator of Christians. I must confess some deep, inside fear about stepping out of that comfort zone. Without Carol's confidence in my writing, I doubt I would have attempted this task. Carol carries the heavy end of the log because of my poor penmanship and poor vision. She stands out as one who uses her unusual talents to the cause of the Kingdom of Heaven. Carol wears a dozen hats, at times two or three at once, yet they all adorn a beautiful and Christian personality.

CONTENTS

INTRODUCTION

While I intended this to be a book on apologetics, it is unlike any other I have read. Most apologists write from facts to person, that is, the vector is from the outside in. Whenever possible, I identify with the faulted problem in us all, describe it, and look out toward God and nature from our faulted being.

When God spoke to Cain about his low feelings, He said, "If you do well, will you not be accepted?" appealing to Cain's natural and emotional desire to correct how he felt. God addressed Cain's reasoning ability saying you are your own problem, not Abel or your parents. You are not feeling comfortable because of error in your antecedent behavior.

Such is the intrinsic nature of the creature man, that evidence for Ultimate Being from outside man is evidence in the sphere of objectivity. Most apologists tend to ignore the viewing subject, which is exactly where this book takes acute focus. The unbeliever is not in harmony with facts about others, especially The Other.

Unbelievers have no values beyond natural death so I attempted to write to them from the here and now to the cemetery. I have no conscious problem identifying with the unbeliever. I began life a purebred sinner with certified papers and my psyche wears scars of my many personal sins. In Adam, I too had a great fall. In Christ, I pray unbelievers will sense evidence of a return for me toward "image" and "likeness." I cannot believe that man can completely obliterate all likeness and image of God nor make the complete 180-degree turn to original Divine intent.

I understand how dead being dead in sin really is, yet the Spirit is out there as surely as Satan and culture is out there. I write to man just as I find him. My focus is his mind and heart, that is his emotions. The warnings of Sacred Scripture are also sacred. Scriptures are revealed, not discovered by science from created things. They are spirit so I do not, to the best of my being, appreciably anthropomorphize them. I have borrowed from philosophers and theologians who demonstrated a reach toward God with the arms of their mind and heart. Still, the reasoned conclusions are my own, perhaps to a fault. I have written of the concepts of altruism that have guided me in the service of caring for many decades. I pray I can help the unbeliever identify himself, unchained by an inordinate ego, with rebellious frosting covering it.

My thesis is very simple: To deny ultimate reality is to travel the road of exclusive human rationality into nihilism. To deny God as ultimate reality is to travel the road of exclusive human reason into hell, as if nihilism was not already man's worst consequence.

In the realm of the logical mind, just one step into cultural relativism is a step toward the non-being in nihilism. In this book, I purpose to follow deductive logic and argue that to depart from God as our major premise assures faulted conclusions. Creature freedom, independent of a Creator, is not freedom at all; it is dangerous insanity. Insanity is exclusively a creature experience. It is one of creature man's original creations.

CHAPTER 1
What Is Smart?

I once was asked by the League of Women Voters to speak to them on the subject of rape, at a large gathering at the University of Arizona. I had been involved in what is called a high-profile rape case. Rape is a violently intrusive invasion of a woman's soul and body.

Upon completion of my talk, there was a question-and-answer session. A young woman of hippie persuasion stood and asked, "What right have you to talk about rape? Have you ever raped or been raped?" It is the young lady's logical analysis (or the lack of such) that I wish to discuss. She went on to express that it was not my legal right to be present that she was questioning, but my rational qualification, since I was outside the paradigm of rapist/victim. She missed the whole psychological approach of inductive/deductive reasoning and the formal language of logical analysis.

I was more dramatically involved than the young lady guessed, for I analyzed evidence in the case as to the rapist's identity from the crime scene study and interviews. He was arrested and went to prison. The young lady was tall, pretty, and passionately sincere. She was not totally out in left field academically, and may have read something of Edmund Husseri's phenomenological reduction theory. This theory puts together all that can be consciously known and relates it to one's horizons of personal experience.

The young lady committed what is called in logic the ad hominem abusive fallacy. This means she ignored what I said and deliberately attacked me. (Ad hominem, in Latin, means "against the person.")

She left the meeting as much a potential victim of rape as she was when she came in, because she excluded me with her restricted personal horizon based solely on her experience.

Logic dictates that if she persists, she will not come to ultimate reality, because she dismisses everything and everyone outside her horizon of personal experience. Rape is experienced from the outside inward, but how we understand evidence is often predetermined by the cognitive maze we cement in our head. The dominant equation in this book is not being to being, but Ultimate Being to mortal being.

The simple and sufficient answer to the question posed was that I was invited by the president of the group. That is not the point I wish to make. It was the young hippie's presupposition that only experience gives us the right to share with our fellow human beings. For me, the question of intelligence or a keen mind is not easy to answer. I do hold that belief in God must be quite intelligent and that unbelief is too often the result of faulty reasoning.

Noah Webster, in his 1828 edition of the *American Dictionary of the English Language,* defines intellect thus: "A clear intellect receives and entertains the same ideas which emotion communicates with perspicuity." It follows that if God is and He communicates to us, it could only be with perspicuity. Perspicuity means lucidly clear or understandable. A faulty message could only be in the receiver.

Noah Webster, like Saul of Tarsus, was not a volunteer to the Christian faith, although he became a very strong Christian. In his own words in the introduction to his dictionary cited above, he wrote, "I now began to understand and relish many parts of the Scripture which before appeared mysterious or repugnant to my natural pride." Later on in my book, I will deal with the changing mind that Noah Webster and two others experienced. Just now, I wish to stay with native intelligence, since God says He also speaks to our native minds.

God talks to the unbeliever; He communicates with the believer. This whole book is about being smart enough to stay out of the realm of estrangement from God. The mind plays a central role, and is central to our person, as are our emotions. I chose to address the mind of disbelief, not just its origin at birth, but its personal evolution in each of us. A mind may be a terrible thing to waste, but it is a difficult faculty to evolve so that it becomes comfortable with ultimate reality.

I did share with the rape victim's loved ones. I anguished with them in their mental and emotional experience because I walked naked—but not mindless—into their experience through their opened door into their sphere of being. To walk mindless would have denied them the presence of my being. We were never subjects to objects; never antecedents then consequence. The heavy yoke was upon us all. This, however, is pastoral care, and I must get back to theology and apologetics. Perhaps in my defense, I needed to say life for me does not begin and end with rationality. The young lady opened the door to the limits of human experience, so perhaps I am not defending "too loudly."

At its minimal definition, mind must not disengage from the total being of man.

CHAPTER 2
The Burden of Creatureliness

How did Satan entice Eve over to his egotistical side, as recorded in the Holy Book in Genesis 3:1-6? First, the serpent was smart enough, but that—in and of itself— does not carry a reasonably assured effect. Some soul restlessness at the core of being a *creature* must have been in operation. For theologians, it is difficult to answer how Satan's tactics were effective before sin entered human experience.

My theory, and I can find some support in the Bible, is that creature obedience or disobedience to the Creator is part and parcel of the Creator/creature paradigm, believer or unbeliever notwithstanding. When we get to the New Covenant in Christ's blood and we have the Redeemer/redeemed paradigm, obedience is still with us, and is part and parcel of the paradigm. Once we plant the seed of disobedience, we have the potential for full-fledged rebellion at the next level.

I believe this is the origin of sin or evil, but Eve was not first. Satan and his buddies were first among created beings to sin. Many very devout theologians do not purport to know the origin of evil. Still, evil is a departure from the Creator's intended purpose. I do not know the true truth, but my theory makes a lot of sense, and nothing later in the Bible, to my knowledge, refutes my theory.

God told Moses, "I AM WHO I AM." The word "extant" in English explains God quite well. That is, He is existent and known, or surely can and should/must be known. Man is a created being and when he—man—disobeys, sin is a product. God purposed that sin would result. The renowned Christian scholar, Dr. R.C. Sproul, speaks of any sin as cosmic treason, because it not only disobeys God's moral law, it rebels against God's created cosmic order. Dr. Sproul also has a lot of brilliance in the area of philosophy. He may not agree with my theory of the origin of evil, yet his definition of cosmic treason supports my theory.

Please do not underestimate the intestinal fortitude in man to break the equation of Creator/creature. I have friends who would risk life to break the equation. This saddens me. Still, I have friends who would risk eternity to break the equation. The desire to rid ourselves of God, even to kill Him, is not dead. This engulfs me in tragedy. Early in the Bible, we find a demonstrative example of man's problem with the Creator/creature equation (Gen. 11:1-9). The Tower of Babel, as it came to be called, was built on the plains of Shinar, but the name man wished to obtain was to be found in the heavens. This is where they assumed God achieved His name and advantage over them.

I know of another "Tower of Babel" where the name is no less fitting yet the driving force must be the same. I do not believe this later tower was built with the same predetermined deliberation. The "material" in this tower is words, not thoroughly-baked bricks, but words. In the *Webster Third New International Dictionary*, we find the "self" prefixed 482 times, as in self-determination, self-glorifying, et cetera. In the same dictionary, God is prefixed about forty-five times. One of the definitions of "Babel" in that same dictionary is a "confusion of sense." In reference to God, I counted these three pejorative terms: goddamn (noun), goddamn (verb) and goddamned (adjective). The editors did not permit the creature self to suffer such indignities.

Chapter 3
Created in Divine Image and Likeness

Regardless of your chronological age and all things that measure what we call a "good life," the above proposition should naturally be brought into question. Without any real understanding of just what is this creature we call "man" that God created and the Biblical account of the fall in the next chapter, your encounter with mankind will remain a mystery and a puzzle.

I have never met an unbeliever I did not like to some degree, and I have never met an unbeliever with a firm grip on these two doctrines—that is creation and the fall. I have met a lot of believers who rejected the fall, at least tacitly, and yet did not show confusion about saving faith. I would dare to say that understanding the nature of man is contingent on acknowledging both of these scriptural doctrines; that is, the creation and the fall, in that order. Without acknowledging both these doctrines, reasoned faith in God is impossible, because redemption can only be reasoned from need felt in the depths of the soul and acknowledged by reason.

Psychology will not help you, because psychology is nothing more than an analysis of gathered human phenomenon. Yes, reason is applied in psychology to the gathered phenomenon, but if the Bible is right (and evidence screams that it is right), "All have sinned and fall short of the glory of God" (Rom. 3:23). Psychologists are, and have been, since the inception of the science, gathering data from the wrong human race. John, the apostle of love, hammers home the same point. "If we say that we have not sinned, we make Him a liar, and His word is not in us" (1 John 1:10). Psychology, whether we like to hear it or not, breaks from the Creator/creature equation by its own chosen scientific paradigm and methods, and as such, will always be the prisoner of the creature half of the equation. It is the best-reasoned argument for the book's title. If you limit your rationality to psychology, it will polish the pathway to hell for you and all your disciples.

"Dan, how dare you write such a statement?" I dare because salvation is of the Lord (Heb. 2:1-4). To trust psychology is to reject the Creator/creature, Redeemer/redeemed equation, therefore, it is to reject God's salvation. The human race got off to the most incredible start than even the loyal angels could imagine. The Bible record reads:

> *"Then God said, 'Let Us make man in Our image, according to Our likeness; let them have dominion over the fish of the sea, over the birds of the air, and over the cattle, over all the earth and over every creeping thing that creeps on the earth.' So God created man in His own image; in the image of God He created him; male and female He created them." (Genesis 1:26, 27)*

Likeness was not material likeness, for man was formed from the earth and God is spirit. Representation and comparison must refer to a more central nature of man. Whatever qualities make man a human being—smarts or intelligence, feelings or emotions, and common moral sense—it is these qualities that we like to think set us off from lower forms of life.

Second Corinthians 4:4 teaches us that image of the invisible God is possible in physical form and was perfectly demonstrated in the historical

Jesus. If we trust our senses and our dreams, something terrible must have happened to us between creation and now. That is what the next chapter is about. Just listen to CNN Headline News. Why, oh why, do we give so much press to the worst of man's conduct? Is it because we identify with such behavior? Identity makes listeners. Listeners attract high-dollar commercials. It is good for business, remember?

CHAPTER 4

The Gold in the Equation, Creator/Creature

I remember as a child hearing on the school playground both, "Who do you think you are talking to?" and "Who do you think you are?" I also remember some fights when the questioned student did not answer to the satisfaction of the questioning aggressor.

Analogous to my illustration, what could we reasonably deduce, should the creature genuinely acknowledge the equation?

1. First, you have being created with likeness and image of an Eternal, self-existing Being, not something that evolved from primordial green slime by chance. Chance is nothing, and nothing cannot produce something.

2. As dependent beings, we are not self-sustaining and life would be frightening were it not for a Creator who knew how to build and sustain a marvelous habitat.

I live just a few miles from Biosphere II. Rumor has it that the Biosphere II is in danger of being dismantled and leveled, making an area for high-dollar homes. I placed a phone call there two days ago to learn just what the original structure was intended to verify. A lady told me it was funded by private money to study whether or not man could live in a totally enclosed environment. Toward what ultimate end, she did not say. It was managed for several years by Columbia University, so much genuinely scientific skill must have been employed. When a neighbor and I took the tour in March 1995, the guide asked if anyone knew what Biosphere I was. "The earth, of course," she responded. Columbia University is gone, and for lack of passion or funds, the whole project is now being threatened.

The creature man again showed himself to be second best to the Creator. The Holy Bible tells of God creating the earth *ex nihilo* from nothing outside Himself. Some feat if you can do it. The founders of Biosphere II had not only a life-sized model but all the materials in Biosphere I, yet they lost their passion. Someone is still sustaining Biosphere I, so life is not immediately threatened.

3. To acknowledge the equation is to be identified with created mankind. Pascal said to bet on God because it is a bet you cannot lose. His wager does not carry the commitment God requires. When the historical Jesus came to earth, He identified with the originally-created race in life and death. Identity with the Eternal Savior is for eternity. God, by His very essence, does not bet or He would not be God. He runs no casino that takes bets. Lordship is singular. Sovereign Lordship rejects all competition.

4. There is also the quality of life and meaningful purpose in individual choice. God must like variety. Are we not all different? I enjoy trying to communicate by writing. Others enjoy working on automobiles. The variety that can fall into God's purpose for man seems almost endless. To reject the equation for me requires too much energy and the risk is too high. Blaise Pascal was not all wrong but he structured the wager without conferring with God. The approval of God was not on his wager.

5. Finally, God does not create other gods. Our adjustment to the one God sounds quite possible. Most of us tend to accept ourselves. Is it not reasonable to believe God had acceptability in mind when He stamped the template? Acceptability is part of the good life. It is never found for long outside of the God/man equation. If you have not shared any of the

good life, you have been goofing around at some level lower than that intended for His big-brained creature.

CHAPTER 5

There Are Ashes in the Equation (Creator/creature)

Reason would anticipate that in forming a relationship between non-equals, some rules of engagement would have to be established. When the lower party would not be in existence without the Higher Party, reason would anticipate the Higher Party to move first, publishing the rules of engagement. When the Higher Power created the habitat for the lower power and made that habitat a free gift, reason would anticipate the lower power would receive something like an owner's manual or operator's manual. Reason would dictate that the Higher Power was best qualified, by far, to write the manual.

The owner's manual has "dos" and "do-nots" in that order. The manual usually says: "Read before operating." Cautions are sundry. The Holy Bible is, in many ways, analogous to a book governing rules of engagement with God, and is an operator's manual for life on earth. Early Genesis is not laden with many sundry rules. In Genesis 2:16, 17, after stating to Adam that he, Adam, could eat freely of every tree in the garden except one, the Lord God put absolute prohibition on the fruit of a single tree. It should not have been confusing to the big-brained creature man. It was not.

I write of reason almost as if it were an entity of itself. Reason is best understood as a capacity we have to get in touch with truth. I know of no reason to distinguish reality from truth. There goes that word "reason" again.

Adam did not come to the rules of engagement or the rules of the garden by reason but by direct communication with Divine reality. When Martin Luther spoke of reason as the devil's whore, he was thinking of reason exclusive of God's self-revelation in Christ, Scripture and nature.

Where are the possible ashes in the Creator/creature equation? In Deut. 30:19, 20 we read:

> *"I call heaven and earth as witnesses today against you, that I have set before you life and death, blessing and cursing; therefore choose life, that both you and your descendants may live; that you may love the Lord your God, that you may obey His voice, and that you may cling to Him, for He is your life and the length of your days; and that you may dwell in the land which the Lord swore to your fathers, to Abraham, Isaac, and Jacob, to give them."*

Moses tells that this message was given to him directly by God and in chapter 31, verse 1, speaking in the third person, he wrote, "Then Moses went and spoke these words to all Israel." God was and is never given to euphemisms such as "death is a part of life." Death is a part of life when at the cemetery we say goodbye to loved ones, yet they remain distinct cogent concepts. In Jewish theology, good and life are one and evil and death are one.

> *"Because God is the moral measure of all things, an objective revelation of morality is essential. Thus Moses completes his review of OT law with these words: 'See, I set before you today life and prosperity [tōḇ "good"], death and destruction [ra', "evil"]' (Deut. 30:15). God's written Word communicates*

all we need in order to develop a moral sensitivity that will enable us to know what is good and what is evil." Expository Dictionary of Bible Words. Lawrence O. Richards.[1]

I often use the expression of ashes in the psyche (soul, mind, and spirit), but ashes in the eternal soul of man are unthinkable for me. Let's studiously avoid it.

CHAPTER 6

Adam! Adam! We Had a Great Fall

I am sure some of you readers will ask, "Dan, are you not confused about the pronoun *we?*" You could not have been there and have participated in Adam's sin and disobedience. Does not Genesis 3:6 read, "So when the woman saw that the tree was good for food, that it was pleasant to the eyes, and a tree desirable to make one wise, she took of its fruit and ate. She also gave to her husband with her, and he ate"? Before I answer the question, may I point out the role of the natural senses for Eve? The fruit was good for food. It was pleasant to the eyes. Finally, it held out the promise of becoming wise, godlike, that is. Sounds safe so far, doesn't it? The problem is, it broke the equation of Creator/creature, those rules of engagement that the unequal equation requires. She made a creature judgment that had already been determined by Ultimate Being and she was a created being. David said, "Know that the Lord, He is God; It is He who has made us, and not we ourselves" (Ps. 100:3a). The right of creatorship extends to all creation.

Theology has a big word when it talks of the role of Adam and Eve's relationship to the human race. God ordained that Adam and Eve would be the progenitors of the human race. A progenitor is a biologically related ancestor. That is, He would deal with us all by representation. Before you go into a rage because it offends your sense of justice, there is a positive side to God's decision. St. Paul wrote, in 1 Cor. 15:22, "For as in Adam all die, even so in Christ all shall be made alive." God did not change the rule of representation between the Old Testament and the New Testament.

It was Adam and Eve who broke the love-life covenant. Does God love unconditionally? The answer is an unequivocal "No!" That is the kind of devil-inspired reasoning that leads to hell. (It may be inspired, but it is inspired by Satan.)

Adam and Eve accepted the sole prohibition and there is no record that they questioned God about it. The invasive questions directed against God's covenant with Adam and Eve did not originate with either of them. It did not originate in their faculty of reason. They were stand-in actors to a bright angel. You will remember that reason and/or rationality is not the same as a truth. Reason is the faculty of a human mind that God put there to help us touch or get connected with truth. Doubt of God's Word is the abrasive material on the gears of the mind. Satan did not make Eve sin, he just made it easier for her to do so. He bewitches her reasoning process.

So where is the lesson from the historical fall seeing we are already in the deep soup? God is a moral God requiring behavior that distinguishes right from wrong. For many, many centuries, logic has always referred to right or wrong, a judgment by the person. The meaning from logic has always been making a judgment, whether or not you like that word. The creature never takes independent action without breaking the covenant. At any moment, we may feel that we would like to be sovereign, but we never are. When our desire to be sovereign gets out of control, we commit spiritual suicide. All self-determined actions, independent of God, diminish us, not elevate us. If we desire to reason justly, we could conclude that God had every reason to have killed Adam and Eve instantly. This makes God something more than retributive justice. So may we continue our reasoning together?

CHAPTER 7
Major Fallout

Genesis 3:9-19 reports the response of the Lord to the disobedience of our progenitors, Adam and Eve. Someone has said that our courts move too slowly to ever effect justice. In the case of mankind, the court calendar was not jammed. There was no grand jury to determine indictments; no jury was seated; there was no defense counsel. The charge was stated and the defendants pled guilty. The defendants did offer the defense of blaming another. The Judge was unimpressed. The sentence is still with us and in us all. It reads much like a summary judgment.

"Then the Lord God called to Adam and said to him, 'Where are you?' So he said, 'I heard Your voice in the garden, and I was afraid because I was naked; and I hid myself.' And He said, 'Who told you that you were naked? Have you eaten from the tree of which I commanded you that you should not eat?' Then the man said, 'The woman whom You gave to be with me, she gave me of the tree, and I ate.' And the Lord God said to the woman, 'What is this you have done?' The woman said, 'The serpent deceived me, and I ate.' So the Lord God said to the serpent: 'Because you have done this, you are cursed more than all cattle, and more than every beast of the field; on your

belly you shall go, and you shall eat dust all the days of your life. And I will put enmity between you and the woman, and between your seed and her Seed; He shall bruise your head, and you shall bruise His heel.'

To the woman He said: 'I will greatly multiply your sorrow and your conception; in pain you shall bring forth children; your desire shall be for your husband, and he shall rule over you.'

Then to Adam He said, 'Because you have heeded the voice of your wife, and have eaten from the tree of which I commanded you, saying, 'You shall not eat of it': 'Cursed is the ground for your sake; in toil you shall eat of it all the days of your life. Both thorns and thistles it shall bring forth for you, and you shall eat the herb of the field. In the sweat of your face you shall eat bread till you return to the ground, for out of it you were taken; for dust you are, and to dust you shall return.'"

It is not my intent to write a short running commentary on God's response to the couple's disobedience. Such commentaries number in the hundreds. The focus of this book is intellect or reason as it relates to belief. This is not to suggest that Eve made a well-reasoned decision to eat of the forbidden tree. Surely, it was not based on physical need.

There is a mystery for me as to how Satan injected Eve with a self-esteem problem before she had acquired a faulted ego. Now we have a faulted ego problem, unbelievers and believers, even those we refer to as saints. I would not have you believe that Sovereignty arbitrarily does what Sovereignty does in some paradigm without concern for His creation, even after the fall. Being capricious is a creature flaw, never a sovereign one.

In verse 15, God tells Satan that he will deliver a bruise to the offspring of Eve but One of her seed will deliver a bruise to his head. In verse 16, Eve will, as all women shall, bring forth young in pain. She will feel the rule of the male. Still in mercy, her sentence is greatly mitigated.

In verses 17-19, Adam will learn of sweat and sore muscles, the force of a negative nature for all of man's life. Hardship will bow him low toward the ground, whence he shall return at natural death. Still, both he and Eve will live under mitigated sentence, but they shall live for a span. Finally, the Seed of Eve will take their and our place in the prisoner's box and receive the death sentence.

Both Jews and Christians place the writing of Genesis at about 1450 BC. Some of God's pronouncements to Adam and Eve are fulfilled but some are pending. Death is a heavy constant. Much in Genesis appeals to reason. Scripture remains God's own reliable and relevant revelation of ultimate reality. That is God Himself.

CHAPTER 8
Death Is the Prosecutor

"The prosecutor is one who instigates or sets in motion the machinery of criminal justice against a person whom he suspects or believes to be guilty of a crime, by laying an accusation before proper authorities." — *Black's Law Dictionary*.

Death is surer than taxes. You can avoid taxes in prison, but death will visit you there with or without an authorized pass from the warden.

One thing is sure about death: It is a total smash-up. Whether our soul/mind goes on functioning after death, science cannot answer. "Mind is often thought to be the last domain that stubbornly resists understanding."[2] *Oxford Dictionary of Philosophy,* Simon Blackburn.

Since this book is about how diminished intelligence can lead to prosecution by death, let's deal in the you-can-know-it sphere. We know we have a body by tactile evidence as that which satisfied Thomas after Christ's resurrection (John 20:28). Pain and pleasure are good witnesses to the mind that the body has being equal unto reality.

For me, the function of body and mind is a fascinating study. As a hospital chaplain in pastoral care, I have ministered to organ recipients. Doctors will harvest your organs, with your pre-determined consent, when you are determined to be brain dead. Do they mean when you are mind-dead, rejecting the dualism of Plato and Descartes? Is it possible, if dualism is reality, that you—that is your soul/mind in some transcendent form or modality—may be watching doctors harvest your organs? Had you lived your life as a selfish, egotistical bastard, you would now be savoring the sweet honey of altruism.

This short book is for you, the unbeliever, and for the Gnostic. What I am trying to point out is that you are an unbeliever and/or Gnostic by way of mind, since you could not have gotten there by way of body and material alone. Mind in body is somehow welded to time. Time and death transcend taxes and death as first among the unavoidables.

The prosecutor death will bring you to trial and he will bring it to you in this sphere we call time. Reality is shouting at you that you do not have forever to decide about God.

Surely you can go down trying. First, kill God in your mind, but the prosecutor death remains. No one tried harder than Nietzsche. In his *The Gay Science,* he tells of the madman who hails it as the greatest achievement of mankind to have killed God and turned the churches into tombs and sepulchers of God. Pity Nietzsche's madman, for the shadow of God cannot be vanquished for people do not listen to a madman. Pity Nietzsche, for while he relegates Christian faith and morals to the misguided and weak, he failed to kill the prosecutor, death. Nietzsche contended that what is good is what is powerful. Should we service violence and trauma as the strong and affirm such as good not evil? His motto was "Let's do it again." We would have hoped, at least for him, that it would have survived the prosecutor. Perhaps from the grave, he shouted, "Let's do that again."

Return with me to death and diminished credence as death's victim. Why listen at all to a being who is going to die? His truth cannot be a universal. My soul laments. Let us all, who are mortal, join hands and have an infinite cry. But in reality, we cannot even achieve that for our crying would be finite. Can you share the requiem? It is the spirit and mind imprisoned for now in a mortal body. If my philosophy be in error, I pray you, tell me how I can have confidence in anyone or anything mortal?

CHAPTER 9

God Draws the Curtain on Eternity

Not being able to accept the harsh reality of our mortality has, perhaps, kept more people out of the eternal Kingdom of Heaven than any single identifiable factor. If we are not going to die, the question of the reality of God becomes a gratuitous question, a question that lacks necessity. It is difficult to evaluate one as sane if the denial of death dominates their best reason.

With the son of Adam and Eve who represented us all, God locked mortal life and eternal life with a chain that no one nor all mortals can break. I use a chain as a metaphor or metonymy to help explain a pronouncement of the Eternal Being. God is really tough on disobedience. "The soul who sins shall die" (Ezek. 18:4). "For all have sinned and fall short of the glory of God" (Rom. 3:23). Whether I quote two or one hundred Bible texts, the element of our reason remains the same. Simply, we lose control of life at death. For mortal man, only the living can influence his life. If you cannot accept the reality of your mortal being, I simply cannot reason with you. You have dropped the steel curtain on the lateral influence of reason. If you do not recognize yourself as a mortal being, a son of Adam, may I suggest you go to the cemetery on a nice day, meditate, and surrender the best of your natural senses to the milieu? As a believer in the eternal reality of God, I have prayed there and walked away unabashed. I have thought of getting drunk in the cemetery, but reason dictates that I would only change my perception of reality, and true reality would remain extant. It would deny me change to ease my mortal uneasiness.

Descriptively speaking only, I feel that sin, or God's condemnation of sin, made the ego so dominant in the human personality that its reason cannot reach toward God. The Word of God says that left to itself, without the help of God's spirit, the ego will not reach Godward at all. That is not to the Judeo-Christian God of Sacred Scripture. To the degree that any mortal can declare, I declare to you that ego sets limits to the reach of the self resulting in disbelief. I have never met an unbeliever whose ego acknowledged its mortality.

My ears can hear some of you say, "Author, you are now getting nasty." I would plead *a priori* that I truly am over-identified with unbelievers. I cannot say something about you that I have not said of myself to God in humble repentance. I deny a subject-object relationship with you.

Satan held out to Eve a promise of godlikeness for the creature, should she decide to oppose God's order. What she got after she trusted to another with an ego problem was this albatross on the soul or self that we have come to call egotism. In the incredibly gifted package of image and likeness, there was something like a compass made in heaven. Now we must carefully guard against faulty reason and all the other faulted parts that promote such. We must daily clean the glass of that compass.

St. Paul lamented upon consideration of his mortal capacity and the need of eternal salvation. "O wretched man that I am! Who will deliver me from this body of death?" (Rom. 7:24). I will attempt God's answer in the next chapter, since none of us since Adam and Eve has avoided death or its coming surety. Unbeliever, if you remain so without resolving the death problem, your mind is still on the dance floor. Would you consider that when the orchestra stops playing, the dance is over forever?

CHAPTER 10

"If a Man Dies, Shall He Live Again?" (Job 14:14)

When I closed the last chapter, I spoke of mortal life being linked with eternal damnation if man was left to his own faulted abilities. I have already quoted Genesis 3:19 and the same statement appears later in the Bible: "And as it is appointed for men to die once, but after that the judgment" (Heb. 9:27). These passages deal with God's judgment of sin. God will never change His position on sin. To think that God would negotiate His holiness can only be the thought of a sinful, faulted mind crying from the pit of desperation. We have not yet looked at a more complete description of God from self-revelation. I never cease to be jolted by people when they tell me they feel God is out to get them. I always try to answer with a compassionate voice, "If God wanted to get you, He would have done it yesterday and we would not be seeking His grace and mercy today."

Moses was the first to leave us a more complete description of God. Moses went up Mount Sinai for the second set of stone tablets containing the Ten Commandments. If it is not insolent, I would say that God privileges Moses to a little cosmic theater, for we read:

> *"Now the Lord descended in the cloud and stood with him there, and proclaimed the name of the Lord. And the Lord passed before him and proclaimed, 'The Lord, the Lord God, merciful and gracious, long-suffering, and abounding in goodness and truth, keeping mercy for thousands, forgiving iniquity and transgression and sin, by no means clearing the guilty, visiting the iniquity of the fathers upon the children and the children's children to the third and the fourth generation.' So Moses made haste and bowed his head toward the earth, and worshiped." (Ex. 34:5-8)*

Some of the problem unbelievers have with the reasonableness of God is the strange concepts they hold of Him. These concepts are not surrendered easily. The big ego, egotism, in the self is singular, and God Almighty is singular, so why are we surprised if there is a clash in their reason? God will not negotiate His person to help us understand, but He will surely help us. If you have lived total life until now without mortal stress about God, you can be sure you have never met Him, nor were you proximate.

There is a lot of history between Moses in the book of Exodus and the New Testament epistle to the Hebrews. Once God gave Moses the Law, someone had to keep it perfect as our representative. We are all sinners, so someone had to die in our place, for "without shedding of blood, there is no remission [of sin]" (Heb. 9:22). The Epistle to Hebrews begins:

> *"God, who at various times and in various ways spoke in time past to the fathers by the prophets, has in these last days spoken to us by His Son, whom He has appointed heir of all things, through whom also He made the world's; who being the brightness of His glory and the express image of His person, and upholding all things by the word of His power, when He had by Himself purged our sins, sat down at the right hand of the Majesty on high." (Heb. 1:1-3)*

It is where God seated His Son that should cause us to trust Him, God opened the curtain on eternity with the sacrifice of Christ for us all (John 3:16).

Peter spoke in Acts while filled with the Spirit, and said, "Nor is there salvation in any other, for there is no other name under heaven given among men by which we must be saved" (Acts 4:12). Do not let anyone misunderstand me on reason. It cannot decide how many ways to God, but by the Spirit, it can lead you to the true One, Jesus Christ of Nazareth, as Peter chose to call Him, "For there is one God and one Mediator between God and man, the Man, Christ Jesus" (1 Tim. 2:5).

Salvation is not doing what none of us can do. Salvation is trusting the One who has done the job for us. Lose the big ego in the desert and trust what God said and did. Be assured: Egotism is only a part of a sinful mortal. It can only accompany you to hell. This life is our only chance and place to lose it. Once it gets you there, it will be stench in the nostrils of your soul. Recognize it as the beast in you that it really is. God is a terrible Being to stay away from.

CHAPTER 11
The Hell of Nihilism

There are two hells to avoid. One is the Biblical hell that I believe spills over into mortal life, and we call the second hell nihilism. The late Paul W. Pruyser, Ph.D., who was with the Menninger Clinic, wrote that "nihilism dwells in senselessness."

Friends, some very close to me and dear to me, remind me of the book I am writing and suggest, "Keep it simple, stupid." The problem with simple is that it is not reality. When we get in touch with reality, it isn't simple.

I would quote a great man of reason who, when he was an atheist, had believers for breakfast, and when converted to Christianity, "feasted" on unbelievers.

> *"A child, saying a child's prayer, looks simple. And if you're content to stop there, well and good. But if you're not—and the modern world usually isn't—if you want to go on and ask what's really happening—then you must be prepared for something difficult. If we ask for something more than simplicity, it's silly then to complain that the something more isn't simple. Another thing I've noticed about reality is that, besides being difficult, it's odd: it isn't neat, it isn't what you*

expect."[3] *C.S. Lewis, The Case for Christianity, Macmillan Publishing Company, p. 36.*

Earlier in the book, I spoke of reality and truth as being joined at the hips. Lewis's thoughts on reality were not new for me upon reading his book. I have held that conviction for decades. I would even dare to say God intended it to be that way. A careful reading of Genesis 3:17-19 strongly implies it is part of God's curse on nature and includes the natural man. That is, man is faulted as nature is faulted.

Nihilism is not a colloquial, common-language term. Still, it is easy to define and understand. It is from the Latin word *nihil* (nothing), a theory that claims there is no meaning and value to life. Hell does not reside in a theory; hell resides in the psyche, when we buy into a godless world view. Bad or dumb reasoning is the antecedent and depression in the soul is the consequence. Nihilism is a product of man's mind that has run itself out. It is usually, if not always, deciding to go it alone without any ultimate truths, reality, or God. It is a mind emptied of life, purpose, or hope. It is more like nothing than anything else is like nothing. It is less than chance, and chance is nothing. It has all the gut feelings of mind and emotional depression. It is as if the whole cosmos has rejected the person. It is difficult to explain something whose meaning is nothing by meanings that are something. Perhaps it is something like an empty mortal being for whom dying sounds better than being alive with a brain that won't serve the soul. (There went my promise of a simple explanation.)

Rick Warren's bestseller, *A Purpose Driven Life,* was an attempt to put something in the void left by such shows as Seinfeld's sitcom, a "show about nothing" that influenced the popular culture and found a great audience.

Some famous thinkers, Jean-Paul Sartre among them, sought positive value in nihilism. He savored the possibility of complete human freedom from God. The first Adam could tell him it wasn't a very original idea. Sartre was sure that man could accept complete moral responsibility for his actions. C.S. Lewis argued that it is an irrational disconnect from ultimate reality that man did not invent. Whatever is ultimately real, we must stay connected or ride the "slippery slope" toward nihilism. Whether the theory or the feeling, nihilism is no more or less than a creature's egotistical determination to go it alone without God. In the last logical analysis, there is either God or there is nihilism.

CHAPTER 12
Who Needs Whom?

Several years ago, I spoke at the Western Interstate Conference on Higher Education at Lake Tahoe. The subject was "Social Casework Based on Client Need." I received the Presidential Committee Citation for the most articulate speaker with the best material. I was a bit embarrassed then and now because I thought the subject was so basic, so obvious, and so elementary. Why would anyone spend taxpayers' funds otherwise?

Now when we come to the Creator/creature equation, guess who the needy party is? I truly dare to say, in fear of God, that if an unbeliever would recognize and acknowledge his creatureliness, he is three-quarters of the way up to the Kingdom of Heaven. Surely, I speak only of the creature realm of man's salvation. Allay your worry about God. He is chasing us. We are not seeking Him, "There is none who understands; there is none who seeks after God" (Rom. 3:11). "I do not need God" is perhaps one of the most childish expressions that the big-brained animal has ever uttered to me. This person who says he does not need God is truly my equal, but I must strongly disagree with his evaluation.

Dr. John Blanchard of England, in his book, *Does God believe in Atheism?*, gives us a nutshell definition of God in the introduction. (Nearly 15 million copies of his publications are in print in more than forty languages.) We will all survive a single-sentence definition of God, I am sure:

> *"Put in a nutshell, I mean 'a unique, personal, plural, spiritual, eternally self-existent, transcendent, immanent, omniscient, immutable, holy, loving Being, the Creator and Ruler of the entire universe and the Judge of all mankind.'"*[4]

There is nothing new or unusual about Dr. Blanchard's attempt to begin a working definition of God unless it be succinct and readable for anyone who reads. Take the term "eternally self-existent." No man can say that about himself because we live off God's earth, else we die sooner than later.

As to being unique in the context of making it without God, we simply are a member of a human race, not one of a kind. "Holy." Who would in good conscience touch this one? I pray it is never me.

There is no point to my going on and on in this vein. Some rulers have aspired to rule the world, but to date, all failed, usually failing in very dramatic destruction.

Allow me to be foolish-minded for just a moment on the subject of self-existence in the modality that God is self-existent: I have no idea how to solve the problem of not dying. Then, there is oxygen. How to make it from nothing outside of our self? Food also grown from nothing outside our self would be a heavy problem. There is the problem of cold and warmth. Where do you dump human waste you cannot dump on God's earth? What about companionship? If you are a male like Adam, how do you create a soft and warm female being who has incredibly exciting form? You may well laugh at me, but I am not insane, and I have not violated Dr. Blanchard's "nutshell" definition of God as he chose to define God. I did not even fill the nutshell.

I have a modest proposal to genuine unbelievers in God: Conquer mortality. This single quality of God may just allow us to petition in His court for a hearing somewhat like Job's most earnest pleas. Our problem is that none of us can match God in a single quality of His Being. We cannot even get close enough to measure accurately.

> *"But indeed, O man, who are you to reply against God? Will the thing formed say to him who formed it, 'Why have you made me like this?'" (Rom. 9:20)*

CHAPTER 13
What About God?

About three decades ago, I was teaching a course in forensic science at Fort Huachuca, an army base in southeastern Arizona. All my students were law-enforcement personnel, whether civil or military. Forensic science is science that is admissible in trial court. Trial court in Arizona is the Superior Court. My material came largely from the work of Douglas Johnson and appeared in *Science Method and Meaning*.[5] The article was entitled, "Mysterious Craters on the Carolina Coast." Professor Douglas set forth six hypotheses to explain the craters. Following a simple inductive method that produced quite simple explanations of possible cause, the class seemed to be with me. Then I went to the deductive and finally critical analysis that each time revealed some hidden weaknesses in our plausible answers. I took the class through the same procedure six times. The class was three hours long, so I did not have to hurry.

All the officers wore weapons with live ammunition, yet amazingly, no one shot me. It was a mentally rigorous three hours. Still it was the kind of training an officer needs to survive in trial court under polarized cross-examination.

There was a well-seasoned homicide detective who always traveled the eighty-some miles to class with me. On our return trip, having traveled about fifty miles, he turned his face toward me and he shouted verbatim, "All right, you son of a bitch, so there is a God!" Need I write that I was stunned since the reality of God or the denial of God was hardly the subject of three hours of lectures. How he reasoned to that conclusion, I do not know. I was afraid to ask. I can only guess that the mental rigors of the lecture showed him that he had not applied a regimen of rigorous enough reason to dispel his doubts about the existence of God.

I have no intention of reviewing from my library, say, *The Logic of Scientific Discovery* by world-renowned Dr. Karl Raymond Popper, or the two volumes of philosophical papers by Imre Lakatos, *The Methodology of Scientific Research Programs* and Volume 2 *Mathematics, Science, and Epistemology* in the hope of changing someone's mind about God's existence. About half of our best scientists believe in God, not because their science proved His existence—but because they *reasoned* to God's existence.

My focus in this book will remain on reason and the annihilating effects of egotism. God, the Father, is Spirit, and Spirit is not in the realm of science. It should not even be an issue of science. It is without, outside. Science deals with created stuff and how created stuff performs and why. It is easy in science to commit the logical fallacy of denying the Antecedent. Evolutionary theory grants to nature a form of self-existence science cannot prove is earned.

Believers believe that God is the cause that created the stuff for scientists and the Ultimate Eternal Being that made human beings who would later be called scientists.

The Bible has some stern warnings about just going on and ignoring what we might learn if we chose to give it our reasoned attention:

> *"For the wrath of God is revealed from heaven against all ungodliness and unrighteousness of men, who suppress the truth in unrighteousness, because what may be known of God is manifest in them, for God has shown it to them. For since*

the creation of the world, His invisible attributes are clearly seen, being understood by the things that are made, even His eternal power and Godhead, so that they are without excuse, because, although they knew God, they did not glorify Him as God, nor were thankful, but became futile in their thoughts, and their foolish hearts were darkened, professing to be wise, they became fools" (Rom. 1:18-22).

CHAPTER 14
Some More Talk about Reason

Many years ago, when I headed up criminal offender rehabilitation, I was approached to sit on committees to determine sanity or insanity. One criterion, somewhat my own, that I used among many was whether or not the client or offender believed that what he said was true or reality by the very fact that he said it. I am caused to say that these clients were using reason; however, their reason was too simple to get along in a complex society, let alone in an attempt to reach for or touch ultimate reality.

In this post-Christian culture, I would have to drop this criterion from consideration because so many believe in relativism, especially when it comes to knowing or acknowledging God.

Relativism is not difficult to understand. It simply states that if something is true for the one who believes it to be true, then it is truth or reality. If I believe in God, then God exists for me, and if you do not believe in God, then God does not exist for you. In other words, the reality of God is determined by the faulted creature's reason. Such philosophical reasoning makes man bigger than God. In fact, man determines if God exists. The pot is saying to the potter, "I do not know you" (Rom. 9:20, 21).

I find such reasoning more childish than I find it insane. Such reasoning fits well the dictionary's definition of infantilism. I once told my very young granddaughter that it was not true that horses liked bacon to eat and got cross-referenced with "Tis too."

The Creator/creature equation does not allow the creature to determine if God exists or if He can exist. Natural science cannot determine God nor prove by scientific methodology if God exists or not. God can only be reasoned from reality that science can classify from creation by taxonomy.

I strenuously disagree with Henry N. Weiman, a rational empiricist, who says that God can be perceived and known in the same sense that any other perceptual object is observed. I wish Dr. Weiman had been born at the time of the historical Christ: His theory of perceiving empirical reality would have been valid.

There are some interesting statements about God recorded in the Gospel of John, (John 14:8), where Philip asks Jesus to show him and the disciples the Father. Jesus told Philip that he had reasoned to the wrong theory of perception because the Father had been right there with them and they both saw Him and did not perceive that they saw Him. The Creator determines the "science" necessary to see Ultimate Reality. That is Ultimate Being, not the creature.

> *"Philip said to Him, 'Lord, show us the Father, and it is sufficient for us.' Jesus said to him, 'Have I been with you so long, and yet you have not known Me, Philip? He who has seen Me has seen the Father; so how can you say, 'Show us the Father'? 'Do you not believe that I am in the Father, and the Father in Me? The words that I speak to you I do not speak on My own authority; but the Father who dwells in Me does the works. Believe Me that I am in the Father and the Father in Me, or else believe Me for the sake of the works themselves'"* (John 14:8-11).

I find no fault with Philip's question; at that moment, Philip would qualify as a rational empiricist of the school of Henry W. Wieman. Philip simply wanted to see the Father in the same sense that any other perceptual object is observed.

Christ did give Philip a lesson worthy of his quest for reality, but it was a lesson in philosophy, not physical science. More specifically, it was in a branch of philosophy called ontology. Ontology studies the nature and structure of reality, in this case, the science of being. You may well argue that the lesson was in metaphysics. Academicians often appear to be guilty of academicism, a sort of pedantic quality that does not easily reveal a desire to teach the general public. They quote other Ph.D.s but very rarely a "blood-pumping oxygen-inhaling" rational layman. The language they use assures them a valid defense. Not one full day has passed since a church friend leveled that very charge at me.

CHAPTER 15
Out-of-the-Head Rationality

Rationality is not difficult to understand. It is simply an expanded definition for reason that I attempted to define as a faculty of the human mind. It's a human capacity to reach for or get in touch with truth and reality. The dictionary specifically defines rationality as the possession or exercise of reason. There is an implied question of whether or not we have reason.

Both unbelievers and believers have rationality, but that is where the similarity separates. Using a simple dictionary definition, we must guard against secular rationalism, the principle of accepting reason as the supreme authority on matters of belief, opinion, and conduct. There is a false doctrine that human reason, unaided by divine revelation, is an adequate or the sole guide to all attainable religious truth. Now that is straight from the Random House *Webster's College Dictionary*. It is not preaching, nor is it from a preacher's book. In the strict sense, it is not equal to a philosophical definition, because you do not have to read through the variances of, say, Descartes, Leibnitz, Hume, and Locke—to mention just four among many. Philosophers rarely just write their definition and drive off. With their definition, they may well begin with Plato and walk you through history, until in confusion, you return to a good English dictionary.

Believers or Christians deny rationalism as the sole road to truth about God, the cosmos, and finally, a most personal faith unto salvation. For me, rationalism is the "Miracle Grow" in the fertile soil of secularism. Surely, it marches in step with the post-Christian culture. As I have argued earlier, it is the broad road to nothing; that is, nihilism. Secular rationalism is not tied to anything eternal. Secular rationalism is not tied to any ultimate reality. Logic allows me to say that when a man dies, he is locked outside the eternal. Without God, Eternal Being, man is dead at death. Dead is dead in this context, so dead is nothing, and nothing is not something. Dead is the nothing of nihilism. In this sense, the unbeliever is rational and shares rationality with the believers. In ultimate reality and ultimate purpose, which is God eternal, created being is found only in God which is never separated from God.

Earlier in the book, I talked about our fall in the first Adam. Theology uses the word, really a doctrine, of total depravity. It is not easy for reason to lift this heavy doctrine. Reason cannot deal with the concept of being hopelessly lost in and of ourselves unless God steps in and helps. In good theology, man is separated from God because of willful rebellion, which is sin. The worst sinner cannot erase image and likeness completely. Man is never, never *nothing*. This makes the philosophy of nihilism a lie. Even in experiencing the horror of God's just wrath even unto hell itself, man is still a real being. It is happening to someone, who is a real being, who cannot be reduced to a non-being.

Rationality will be with all who are creatures of the sole Creator. Even if rationality cannot be demonstrated in a damaged body or in insanity, rationality will remain in the eternal soul with God or separated from God. God will be the determinant, not rationalism of any mortal being.

The following words are recorded from the lips of the Eternal One:

> *"There was a certain rich man who was clothed in purple and*
> *fine linen and fared sumptuously every day. But there was a*
> *certain beggar named Lazarus, full of sores, who was laid at*

his gate, desiring to be fed with the crumbs which fell from the rich man's table. Moreover, the dogs came and licked his sores. So it was that the beggar died, and was carried by the angels to Abraham's bosom. The rich man also died and was buried. And being in torments in Hades, he lifted up his eyes and saw Abraham afar off, and Lazarus in his bosom. Then he cried and said, 'Father Abraham, have mercy on me, and send Lazarus that he may dip the tip of his finger in water and cool my tongue; for I am tormented in this flame.' But Abraham said, 'Son, remember that in your lifetime you received your good things, and likewise Lazarus evil things, but now he is comforted and you are tormented. And besides all this, between us and you there is a great gulf fixed, so that those who want to pass from here to you cannot, nor can those from there pass to us.' Then he said, 'I beg you therefore, father, that you would send him to my father's house, for I have five brothers, that he may testify to them, lest they also come to this place of torment.' Abraham said to him, 'They have Moses and the prophets; let them hear them.' And he said, 'No, father Abraham; but if one goes to them from the dead, they will repent.' But he said to him, 'If they do not hear Moses and the prophets, neither will they be persuaded though one rise from the dead.'" (Luke 16:19-31)

CHAPTER 16
Believer's Rationality

Allow me to be upfront and state that the believer's rationality I write about in this short chapter is in the tradition of the Judeo-Christian faith, not any other major or minor world religion. For now, I will leave in place the definition of God by Dr. John Blanchard I used earlier:

> *"Put in a nutshell, I mean 'a unique, personal, plural, spiritual, eternally self-existent, transcendent, immanent, omniscient, immutable, holy, loving Being, the Creator and Ruler of the entire universe and the Judge of all mankind.'"*[6]

As I stated previously, there is nothing unusual about this definition of God unless it be the author's clarity and brevity. The believer does not begin his reason independent of "In the Beginning, God" (Gen. 1:1). This means rationally that before beginning began, God already existed from eternity. Time is a human attempt at understanding. The believer accepts and acknowledges that he is not self-existing. He fears rebellion because of the high risk of separation from God. Believers are big on acknowledging the antecedent of logical thinking.

Christians do not believe that rationality, however sincere, outside of God will grasp truth unto salvation. Christians do not place faith in reality that is not linked to ultimate reality. Christians do not believe we could know reality were it not for ultimate reality. Christians do not believe we could be true beings were it not for Ultimate Being. This is more sound logic than it is faith. There is nothing wrong with having some well-reasoned factor in logic unless you decide to limit rationality to the autonomous self. Restated, Christians do not believe in autonomy of the created person as having the capacity to develop a satisfactory world view.

Christians must begin with self, the rational being, as does the unbeliever. When rationality is in place and exercised, God is always the major premise. This is possible because God's curse on sin did not destroy totally image and likeness to the degree that there is no God-given rationality. St. Paul, in his epistle to the Romans, declares the possibility of human rationality from the created cosmos. Even given this truth, we cannot reach the definition of God quoted above.

> *"For the wrath of God is revealed from heaven against all ungodliness and unrighteousness of men, who suppress the truth in unrighteousness, because what may be known of God is manifest in them, for God has shown it to them. For since the creation of the world His invisible attributes are clearly seen, being understood by the things that are made, even His eternal power and Godhead, so that they are without excuse, because, although they knew God, they did not glorify Him as God, nor were thankful, but became futile in their thoughts, and their foolish hearts were darkened. Professing to be wise, they became fools." (Rom. 1:18-22)*

I would point out that even this limited knowledge of God was not the result of man's autonomous rationality faulted by sin. God left evidence knowable to man's natural senses and reason in His creation. I believe we can know these invisible attributes about God from the goodness we can see even in unbelievers. We all are part of creation. The unbeliever can demonstrate moral goodness toward his fellow man. He can create great beauty in art. He can design and install air conditioners in our home in the Southwest desert so we can be comfortable in 110-degree heat. The sole point I wish to make is that we are all images of the original Designer.

Since we are totally dependent upon God, we are not rightly related to God unless we are totally surrendered to God. This in no way denies us uniquely individual being and likeness; it enhances it. I sense a disturbing aura in unbelievers as if in their egotism they feel quite distinct from creation.

Also we can obscure image and likeness beyond recognition as Paul reveals in the Biblical text quoted above. There is a point in our rebellion of image and likeness against God where God withholds His invisible hand and the true cancer in our faulted human nature bears hideous fruit.

I taught criminal psychopathology at the University of Arizona and did special studies and worked with psychopaths. I am not just a spectator in the academic stands. I have been a gladiator in the sands of evil life. I faced death that would have entertained psychopathic clients had they followed through. To my highly literate readers, I would write again I do not equate experience with proving truth. I think of experience as that which is analogous to studies in truth. It can cast light on truth and our rationality process. It helps your rationality if you stay alive.

CHAPTER 17
Believers Rationality II

In Believers Rationality I, I spoke of the Judeo-Christian tradition of reality. The Jewish concepts of rationality demanded something firmer than Greek rationality. They demanded time space events that are set in history. Note how the epistle to the Hebrews begins. We don't know who wrote it, but we are sure to whom it was written.

> *"God, who at various times and in various ways spoke in time past to the fathers by the prophets, has in these last days spoken to us by His Son, whom He has appointed heir of all things, through whom also He made the worlds; who being the brightness of His glory and the express image of His person, and upholding all things by the word of His power, when He had by Himself purged our sins, sat down at the right hand of the Majesty on high" (Heb. 1:1-3).*

I have been arguing for reality-anchored rationality over against creature-autonomous rationalism that begins with man and ends up as nothing. Christian or believer rationality attempts to touch God, and there is a lot of evidence that God has already visited us. There is a saying among Jewish believers: "Everyone needs a Rabbi." I desire to lend my voice to their confession. The Jewish believers deny any dichotomy between earth and heaven in reference to ultimate truth.

Dr. Francis A. Schaeffer, founder of L'Abri Fellowship in Switzerland, spoke of the connectedness of rationality between God and finite man.

> *"On the side of infinity, as we saw before, we separated from God entirely, but on the side of personality we are made in the image of God. So God can speak and tell us about Himself— not exhaustively, but truly. (We could not, after all, know anything exhaustively as finite creatures.) Then He has told us about things in the finite created realm, too. He has told us true things about the cosmos and history. Thus, we are not adrift."[7]*
> *Escape from Reason, Francis A. Schaeffer, Intervarsity Press, 1968, p. 83*

Christian rationalism demands a unity of thought between God and man, between heaven and earth. "Your kingdom come, Your will be done, On earth as it is in heaven" (Matt. 6:10). These are the words of God in the flesh to the request of His disciples: "Teach us to pray." God in the flesh was the historical Jesus. The Greek name Jesus is from the Hebrew, meaning "Yahweh is salvation." No finite being can know the will of heaven without the help of God. God can help us with the "true truth." I borrowed that expression from Dr. Schaeffer.

The believer accepts that God's self-relation is the *sine qua non* for true truth in real reality. It is an indispensable factor in knowing God. Believers do not begin with the creature deciding if the Creator exists or not. Believers want to know how to stop the rebellion that began with the first Adam.

The general self-revelation, as it is called in theology, is creation and what remains of likeness and image in our personality. Special revelation is Scripture, the written account:

"All Scripture is given by inspiration of God, and is profitable for doctrine, for reproof, for correction, for instruction in righteousness" (2 Tim. 3:16).

God intended that select holy men, not perfect men, would record the infinite yet while being finite.

Believers accept Christianity as having the sole comprehensive worldview. Believers do not reject reason, nor do we reject philosophy. It has been a long time since Plato (470-399 BC), whose writing has caused believers to pause and take notice. But Plato and all the philosophers who followed him until today have not conceived of Ultimate Being equal to John Blanchard's brief definition of Ultimate Being. Philosophy has helped many in their exercise of serious rationality before converting to Christianity. St. Augustine in his *Confessions* clearly states this.

I wish to pose an "eyeball-to-eyeball" question to unbelievers. If Plato, and no one since him, found God by sole autonomous self-rationality, however sincere, how long do you anticipate hanging around until you or someone else finds God by this self-determined modality? I truly try to avoid that haunting reality of death or mortality, but Poe's black raven will not take flight afar from my door.

CHAPTER 18

Belief and Rationality (The Old Testament)

When it comes to Christian faith or belief, there is no carte blanche faith. There is no unconditional autonomy granted the creature being in approaching the Creator Being. I have been guilty of writing as if the reader had a good rational grasp of what belief or faith is all about. For our purpose, there is no reason that I am aware of to separate the two concepts. I will use them interchangeably.

The biblical meaning of faith is very precise, but I rarely hear it outside—or inside—of church. The Bible knows nothing about a leap into the unknowable. That came to us from the existential philosophy of Sören Kierkegaard (1813-1855). Faith based on biblical rationality does not play jump. God hates jumping into the unknown and God rivals no unknown gods. St. Paul had an experience at Athens that I believe should help us dismiss the unknown from Christian faith.

> *"Then certain Epicurean and Stoic philosophers encountered him. And some said, 'What does this babbler want to say?' Others said, 'He seems to be a proclaimer of foreign gods,' because he preached to them Jesus and the resurrection. And*

they took him and brought him to the Areopagus, saying, 'May
we know what this new doctrine is of which you speak? For
you are bringing some strange things to our ears. Therefore we
want to know what these things mean.' For all the Athenians
and the foreigners who were there spent their time in nothing
else but either to tell or to hear some new thing. Then Paul
stood in the midst of the Areopagus and said, 'Men of Athens,
I perceive that in all things you are very religious; for as I was
passing through and considering the objects of your worship,
I even found an altar with this inscription: TO THE
UNKNOWN GOD. Therefore, the One whom you worship
without knowing, Him I proclaim to you: God, who made
the world and everything in it, since He is Lord of heaven
and earth, does not dwell in temples made with hands'" (Acts
17:18-24).

The passion for the new also drives our contemporary culture. Dr. Blanchard's definition of God contained the word "immutable," which means *unchangeable.* The contemporary culture was not the first to have the new, wow, and now tantalizing fantasy. Athenians beat us to it, so it is no longer new. We cannot make the old new; we can only attempt to renew the already old.

People use the word *faith* today like a prayer. "Dear God, bring about what is possible but so very uncertain." The Bible uses faith to connect us with what is assured and faith is not in the evidence that allows the rationality of vector to point to God. Faith is confidence and trust in an Ultimate Being who is God Himself.

"And he [Abraham] believed in the Lord, and He accounted it to him for righteousness" (Gen. 15:6). To understand faith rationally, we must acknowledge that Abraham was certain and assured that God was the object of his faith. Old Testament faith always affirms certainty, never doubt. It always affirms conviction in whom reliability is centered.

Anything that is outside the person Being of God or Christ that gives buoyancy to your faith subjectively or objectively, including so-called evidence, falls short of the biblical definition of faith. When we have faith in God, it is the nature and being of who God is that makes for certain and sure reality.

There is not a hint in the Old Testament that any finite autonomous being will decide if God is what He is in essence or if anyone outside of God Himself will decide what faith is. The finite being who decides to make all these decisions for himself is playing with the fires of hell, seeing that God says he is already condemned. Our autonomous rationality can be the very matches that burn our house down. In the context of faith and rationality, everyone who starts heretical fires burns in his own house. My, how this contrasts the words of "Yahweh is Salvation." "In My Father's house are many mansions" that shall never burn down. (John 14:2).

CHAPTER 19
Belief and Rationality (The New Testament)

If the reader is hoping to find in the New Testament an easier definition of faith that requires less of a commitment and that allows a lot of self-autonomy to be retained, this is not the Testament to search.

The New Testament requires more than acknowledgment toward God. It requires investment in or unto Christ. The Greek preposition "eis" means *to* or *unto Christ*. It is precise. How many ways to God? Who says many ways are possible?

"Thomas said to Him, 'Lord, we do not know where You are going, and how can we know the way?' Jesus said to him, 'I am the way, the truth, and the life. No one comes to the Father except through Me. If you had known Me, you would have known My Father also; and from now on, you know Him and have seen Him.' Philip said to Him, 'Lord, show us the Father, and it is sufficient for us.' Jesus said to him, 'Have I been with you so long, and yet you have not known Me, Philip? He who has seen Me has seen the Father; so how can you say, 'Show us the Father'? Do you not believe that I am in the Father, and

51

the Father in Me? The words that I speak to you I do not speak
on My own authority; but the Father who dwells in Me does
the works. Believe Me that I am in the Father and the Father
in Me, or else believe Me for the sake of the works themselves.'"
(John 14:5-11)

The language is stunning and sobering to our rationality. Notice that you cannot get around Christ to God. Please also notice that in the quote above believing because of miracles is a step down the ladder of faith from faith into Christ Himself. We all want to know the artist after we appreciate his art. God's self-revelation is in His Son. God Himself set Jesus in this position before us, and none other, as the One in whom we must have faith and entrust for the eternal salvation of our souls. Jesus is the Angel of the Lord blocking Balaam's path to self-autonomy. His donkey, a jenny, saw His drawn sword and froze in place (Num. 22:22-34).

Self-autonomy will suffer less when we trust in and to Christ. Unless you are very different from me, you would not be giving up much. Again, the old bugaboo of the undeniable time-space reality of our life confronts us. Self-autonomy can make us less smart than Balaam's jenny ass.

God decided that life is available only through the Son.

"Most assuredly, I say to you, he who hears My word and
believes in Him who sent Me has everlasting life, and shall
not come into judgment, but has passed from death into life"
(John 5:24).

"Therefore I said to you that you will die in your sins; for if you
do not believe that I am He, you will die in your sins" (John
8:24).

The number of times I quote Christ is not relevant to the reality of His words. The New Testament knows of no saving faith that is outside of Christ. "Trusting God is the heart and soul of faith that centers in our Lord Jesus Christ" (Lawrence O. Richards)[8]

The God-man who said there is only one way to God proved His sincerity with the seal of His life. Pilate posted guards at the tomb to prove His words wrong and sealed the tomb with a stone (Matt. 27:65-66). That is a well-documented historical event.

CHAPTER 20
Rationality of One Way to God

Some of you may say, "Dan, if you are so certain there is only one way to God, and that way is Christ, why are you writing further on the subject?" First, I am writing to unbelievers, most of whom hold that even if there is one God, they have every right to choose the route. Secondly, I honor God by attempting to understand His great works among us, and one of the greatest works is the sending and the coming of Christ in the flesh like our own flesh.

"In the beginning was the Word, and the Word was with God, and the Word was God. He was in the beginning with God. All things were made through Him, and without Him nothing was made that was made. In Him was life, and the life was the light of men. And the light shines in the darkness, and the darkness did not comprehend it. There was a man sent from God, whose name was John. This man came for a witness, to bear witness of the Light, that all through him might believe. He was not that Light, but was sent to bear witness of that Light. That was the true Light which gives light to every man coming into the world. He was in the world, and the world was made through Him, and the world did not know Him.

He came to His own, and His own did not receive Him. But as many as received Him, to them He gave the right to become children of God, to those who believe in His name: who were born, not of blood, nor of the will of the flesh, nor of the will of man, but of God. And the Word became flesh and dwelt among us, and we beheld His glory, the glory as of the only begotten of the Father, full of grace and truth." (John 1:1-14)

Every man born (man or woman) since Adam was born in sin and under a death sentence. David wrote, "Behold, I was brought forth in iniquity, and in sin my mother conceived me" (Ps. 51:5). We may argue about when life begins, but there is no argument when changeable sinners begin. How did God help us?

The concept of redemption is an Old Testament one and required a kinsman family member to buy one back (Lev. 25:47-51). If you wanted to be a kinsman redeemer, you had to be family and rich enough to buy back your relative sold into slavery. The Bible represents us all as sold into the slavery of sin. That is why Jesus had to become a member of the human race by way of being born of a natural woman. Had He been born of man and woman He would have been born a sinner like us all. "For all have sinned and fall short of the glory of God" (Rom. 3:23). Not only was Jesus born without sin and did not sin, He challenged His religious enemies to dare convict Him of sin. Do not ever make such a challenge, not even to friends (John 8:46). There were many accusations, but none of personal sin. Christ was qualified to be our kinsman redeemer by birth into the human race. By a sinless life, He became an acceptable holy sacrifice unto God for the sins of us all.

St. Paul, in his letter to the Ephesians, explains just what Christ did for us in our helpless situation.

"But God, who is rich in mercy, because of His great love with which He loved us, even when we were dead in trespasses, made us alive together with Christ (by grace you have been

saved), and raised us up together, and made us sit together in the heavenly places in Christ Jesus, that in the ages to come He might show the exceeding riches of His grace in His kindness toward us in Christ Jesus. For by grace you have been saved through faith, and that not of yourselves; it is the gift of God, not of works, lest anyone should boast. For we are His workmanship, created in Christ Jesus for good works, which God prepared beforehand that we should walk in them." (Eph. 2:4-10)

Your emotions may be repelled by the thought of a bloody human sacrifice offered to God. Yet, either Christ died for you or you will die in your sins to the peril of your eternal soul. It is a take-it-or-leave-it Divine offer. Seize it. You cannot sacrifice yourself for your sins by the very fact that you are a sinner. God would not accept the blood sacrifice of yourself. St. Peter put it very plainly:

"but with the precious blood of Christ, as of a lamb without blemish and without spot. He indeed was foreordained before the foundation of the world, but was manifest in these last times for you who through Him believe in God, who raised Him from the dead and gave Him glory, so that your faith and hope are in God." (1 Pet. 1:19-21)

But you say, "Dan, you promised us a rationale for the one and only way to God." Here it is: Since all sin is rebellion against a Holy God, He alone sets the criterion for recovery. He who is the Judge of the whole world said it was Christ alone, and demonstrated to us that Jesus is trustworthy with the historical resurrection. Were you a defendant in a trial court and found guilty, you would not dream of asking the judge if he exists, nor declare your right to determine sentence. God has only one Begotten Son to offer up for us.

"The next day, John [the Baptist] saw Jesus coming toward him, and said, 'Behold! The Lamb of God who takes away the sin of the world! This is He of whom I said, 'After me comes a Man who is preferred before me, for He was before me. I did not know Him; but that He should be revealed to Israel, therefore I came baptizing with water.' And John bore witness, saying, 'I saw the Spirit descending from heaven like a dove, and He remained upon Him. I did not know Him, but He who sent me to baptize with water said to me, 'Upon whom you see the Spirit descending, and remaining on Him, this is He who baptizes with the Holy Spirit.' And I have seen and testified that this is the Son of God.'" (John 1:29–34)

CHAPTER 21
Sin in the Psyche

If you are an unbeliever, would you hear me out on some interpersonal reasons to walk into the new creation? Earlier in the book, I wrote of my work with psychopathic offenders and that I taught criminal psychopathology at the University of Arizona Graduate College. As long as I live, I expect to remember one serial killer I befriended, to the degree that he desired to ask me a confidential question of great personal concern to him. The question was, "Dan, this conscience thing I hear about. Tell me, is it real or just a technique of the prosecutor to try and break my spirit?"

"It is true for most of us," I said.

The problem of knowing ourselves is very difficult and fraught with frustration. The viewing subject, our self, must view the viewed object, our self. When Flip Wilson used to play Geraldine, his/her line was, "What you see is what you get." A more accurate statement is what you are seeing is what you are, the viewing subject, as well as the viewed object, yourself. Reasonable objectivity takes flight.

Now, given the reality of the great fall in the first Adam, sin entered the viewing subject at its very center. Can you believe Adam's response to God when he was questioned about partaking of the forbidden fruit? "The woman whom You gave to be with me, she ..." (Gen. 3:12) Can you imagine trying that on the God of all creation, especially the One who gave him the gracious mate he called woman, later named Eve? Not smart! The point I wish to make is that he did not become like God; rather, he was greatly cranked down in rationality and in his inner nature. He did not just lose objective perception; his loss was diminished being. He was immediately less than "very good" (Gen. 1:31). There were five assessments of "good." Then came "very good" following man's creation. This was the crown jewel in human creation that we let slip away.

We need to know that God did not buy into Adam's rationalization way back then, and He will not buy into ours, even if we bring it home after a session with a Ph.D. psychologist. Sin in the psyche is more serious than a disease. Sin in the psyche changes our most elemental quality, which was solely of God, to evil like the devil. Medical doctors like to label sin-faulted behavior a disease because that brings it under their medical domain. Yet, in God's sight, it is an integral part of our faulted human nature. The Bible does not know of the person as a subject and sin as a separate subject. The Bible no longer views sin as invasive, but intrinsic to our very nature. That is the truth psychologists cannot live with. It is the truth that literally kills humanism. It was the crucifixion of humanism forever.

Is anyone out there reading me? King David, in his confession to God of his sin with Bathsheba, got past any psychological consideration to concrete reality of sin in his psyche.

> *"Have mercy upon me, O God, according to Your lovingkindness; according to the multitude of Your tender mercies, blot out my transgressions. Wash me thoroughly from my iniquity, and cleanse me from my sin. For I acknowledge my transgressions, and my sin is always before me. Against You, You only, have I sinned, and done this evil in Your sight—that You may be found just when You speak, and blameless when You judge. Behold, I was brought forth in iniquity, and in sin my mother conceived me." (Ps. 51:1-5)*

We must notice that David reasoned all the way back to his conception in his mother's womb and could not separate his being from his sin. Conversion is an acknowledgement of utter helplessness before God, and it is accepting God's remedy of our problem. And just how does God, by His Spirit, do this? He does it with a heart transplant that is an inner nature transplant.

> *"Then I will give them one heart, and I will put a new spirit within them, and take the stony heart out of their flesh, and give them a heart of flesh, that they may walk in My statutes and keep My judgments and do them; and they shall be My people, and I will be their God." (Eze. 11:19-20)*

Another major prophet of the Old Testament, Jeremiah, speaks of an incurable heart disease (Jer. 17:9). To the Hebrews, the heart is at our core being the whole of conscious self. We all have heard of being born again. This is the New Testament expression of what Ezekiel wrote about.

> *"There was a man of the Pharisees named Nicodemus, a ruler of the Jews. This man came to Jesus by night and said to Him, 'Rabbi, we know that You are a teacher come from God; for no one can do these signs that You do unless God is with him.' Jesus answered and said to him, 'Most assuredly, I say to you, unless one is born again, he cannot see the kingdom of God.' Nicodemus said to Him, 'How can a man be born when he is old? Can he enter a second time into his mother's womb and be born?' Jesus answered, 'Most assuredly, I say to you, unless one is born of water and the Spirit, he cannot enter the kingdom of God. That which is born of the flesh is flesh, and that which is born of the Spirit is spirit.'" (John 3:1-6)*

This is how we get out of the first creation with Adam as the head into the new creation where Christ is the Head. Just one more reason why you cannot get around Christ. The bottom line is we are all faulted by sin, and

"Salvation belongs to the Lord" (Ps. 3:8). He can create a lot of new hearts. Can He transplant one in you? It is bloodless surgery. You will not even need any sedative. There is no hospital stay, no rehabilitation time, and no in-home nursing.

CHAPTER 22

The Natural Heart Wears Opaque Glasses

Whenever the Bible speaks of man's natural heart or of natural man, it is speaking of man faulted by the curse of sin. When the Bible speaks of our natural mind, I believe it to be most critical of our unrestricted imaginations. This was man's condition just before the Great Flood. "Then the Lord saw that the wickedness of man was great in the earth, and that every intent of the thoughts of his heart was only evil continually" (Gen. 6:5).

What gets imbedded in the heart usually begins with the senses and enters the mind, then finds its way into the heart. As I had mentioned earlier in the book, I hold, at least as a working definition, that the mind retained more image and likeness than the heart. I view the mind as the door to the heart, yet I hold that a rebellious heart affects the flow of reality—truth—to the mind.

I remember, when teaching a class on scientific theory and methodology to law-enforcement officers, I would raise their ire when telling them that total objectivity in viewing evidence was old science. Science advanced by a quantum leap when brilliant theorists discovered that the scientist is also part of the experiment—I mean as real to the experiment as hypothesis, methodology, apparatus, et cetera.

There is humility involved here, and for the egotistical scientists, a lowering of personal expectations. If this scientific lesson of research is learned and the man truly loves his science, there is the possibility of great rewards.

Now let us bring this over to the subject of this book and see what we find. The passage I quoted from Genesis 6:5 vividly portrays the depth and completeness of human depravity. Deprivation is always the antithesis of God and always opposed to God. I neither have the heart nor the intent to browbeat my fellow man, be he an unbeliever, with 100 more quotes from Scripture. There are many more there than 100.

I simply want to say, with all the compassion I can muster in my soul, "Unbeliever, you are not the objective observer of evidence for God that you think you are and purport to be." Science has become your judge, not me. "Are you saying, Dan, that I cannot will myself to be a completely objective observer?" I am saying exactly that.

"Can the Ethiopian change his skin or the leopard its spots?" (Jer. 13:23a). Man cannot change his intrinsic nature. Allow me to turn the tables on myself. "Can an unbeliever examine evidence for evolution with more passion than a believer?" Yes, I believe he can. "Can the unbeliever be a better scientist when viewing evidence, against evolution?" No, he cannot.

The mortal being who surrenders his passion for individual autonomy, especially in the area of self-determined moral righteousness, is not home free until death. At death comes the surety of God's judgment. Who experienced a more dramatic conversion than Saul to Paul, yet in his letters to the church at Rome, he writes as a convert:

> *"O wretched man that I am! Who will deliver me from this*
> *body of death? I thank God—through Jesus Christ our Lord!*

> *So then, with the mind I myself serve the law of God, but with*
> *the flesh the law of sin." (Rom. 7:24-25)*

You all have heard in trial court or television counsel, whether prosecution or defense, ask the judge, "Your Honor, permission to treat this witness as hostile?"

> *A hostile witness is "a witness who manifests so much hostility*
> *or prejudice under examination in chief that the party who has*
> *called him, or his representative, is allowed to cross-examine*
> *him, i.e., to treat him as though he had been called by the*
> *opposite party." Black's Law Dictionary.*[9]

When, as a cogent being created in the image and likeness of God, we were first confronted with the subject of an Eternal Being, we all were qualified as a hostile witness against our self. To the unbeliever, I ask you to be a sworn witness to truth, especially to yourself. Whether in Las Vegas or Tucson, place your bet on the truth that you cannot take yourself out of the experiment of life that God and Satan are running (Job 1:7-9). As we learn from this oldest book in the Bible, should God withhold His invisible hand, Satan would trash us good.

CHAPTER 23
Your Being Is Proof of God

So very many books on apologetics begin with a defense for believing in the existence of God. This book is not a book on apologetics in the classical sense of the word. This book is about faulted rationality and faulted personalities to such a degree that God does not seem necessary or desirable for a self-autonomous life.

I do not even like writing a defense for the existence of God. I am less sure that God is pleased with the many answers we give unbelievers and ourselves. God begins His book of writing to mankind with "In the beginning, God" (Gen. 1:1). The major premise or logic is a declarative statement upon which all knowable truth is based. Genesis begins as if God is a given that just everyone, created in image and likeness, does know or would know if our brain was turned on. For unbelievers, there are many miracles for you if you pause to think. You will find God at the stop signs in your life. Stop breeding your creature imaginations.

I will write this chapter with a single argument for being: Being is to exist. If you do not exist, how is it that you reject God? The concept of being is not a recent one. Philosophers considered the concept of being and its relationship to reality some five hundred years before Christ. Parmenides headed up the Eleatic School of Greek Philosophy. He developed the concept of "being" in opposition to the philosophy of "becoming" by Heraclitus.

Parmenides's most-quoted concept is "that which is, is." When I was four years old, I understood this, but then, along came philosophy and philosophy classes to seed the brain with doubt and creature free-flying imagination. I wonder if the words of Christ to his disciples are in any way analogous.

> *"Assuredly, I say to you, unless you are converted and become as little children, you will by no means enter the kingdom of heaven." (Matt. 18:3)*

Parmenides reasoned that to think at all, we must postulate something which is, and that which is not cannot be thought, therefore cannot be. Thought without being or being without thought are impossible. If there is being, there must be Ultimate Being in which it is grounded. Rene Descartes's (1596-1650) "I think, therefore I am" follows the same logic. All knowledge must begin with being, "I am, I exist," and all existence must have its foundation in Eternal Existence. If I have being, it is impossible that there not be Ultimate Being. And there is my argument for proof of God.

It was Dr. R.C. Sproul, president of Ligonier Ministries of Orlando, Florida, who finally drove the importance of this home into my hard head. A few years ago, a neurologist did a CAT scan on my head. He told me I have the brain of a young man. I asked, "How is that?" He pointed to the film and said, "Look for yourself; almost no water or air spaces." I never would have guessed that as a youngster, the pejorative names we used had basis in neurological science. I do not remember calling another boy an airhead, or accusing him of having water on the brain, but I remember hearing it. I remember being called a blockhead.

Descartes wrestled with this problem. "If I could have been so certain about something," he asked himself, "and yet later discovered I was wrong, how can I know anything for certain?" Rigorous philosophy caused

Descartes to believe that he must first be certain he exists. He famously declared, "I think, therefore I am." He reasoned that even deception proved existence. By the same logic that gave Parmenides "That which is, is" and Descartes "I think, therefore I am," we can move with sound rationality to the reality of God.

This is the same concept used by God when He told Moses how to identify his sender to the people of Israel as "I AM WHO I AM" (Exodus 3:14). Those five words contain every concept found in Dr. John Blanchard's limited definition of God.

> "Put in a nutshell, I mean 'a unique, personal, plural, spiritual, eternally self-existent, transcendent, immanent, omniscient, immutable, holy, loving Being, the Creator and Ruler of the entire universe and the Judge of all mankind.'"[10]

I find it more than a little interesting that St. Paul quotes a Greek poet when he speaks of our relationship to Eternal Being:

> "...so that they should seek the Lord, in the hope that they might grope for Him and find Him, though He is not far from each one of us; for in Him we live and move and have our being, as also some of your own poets have said, 'For we are also His offspring.'" (Acts 17:27-28)

What this passage logically means is that if we have life in Eternal Being, there is no independent life without Eternal Being.

You can trust that non-being cannot produce being, for from nothing, comes nothing. If you accept God or reject Him, you just proved that you have being. It is a short step of the mind to accept Eternal Being, since nothing short of Eternal Being can create true mortal being. You cannot get something from nothing, because nothing has no essence, by the very fact that it is nothing. From Eternal Being, the big-brained being could have easily reasoned to the reality of being.

CHAPTER 24
Looking Outward for Help

Most of my older readers have, no doubt, enjoyed the series *M*A*S*H* on television. The show featured a group of army doctors and nurses ministering in a mobile army hospital not far from the front lines in Korea. Just now, I glanced up from my desk and there was Alan Alda, as Hawkeye, involved in some joviality or another. The Hallmark Channel still plays the reruns in the afternoon.

The writers of *M*A*S*H* did a great job of mixing the grave reality of war with the best of cockamamie behavior, in the hope of showing survival skills. All of the above is just to get to a point of therapy when, on occasion, Hawkeye would really lose it. There was always the call to Dr. Sidney Freedman, psychiatrist. With delicate free-association and carefully selected pauses, the traumatic horror of past experience was discharged in a dramatic catharsis. Catharsis was seen as occurring when the normal paths of conscious emotions are discharged. Freud thought that emotion (he called this "affect") having been "strangulated" along the normal path leading to consciousness was released in therapy.

As I rudely implied a couple of chapters ago, if the catharsis is not controlled within the framework of socially accepted moral guidelines, even loved ones can be murdered. The catharsis in *M*A*S*H* makes for entertaining script but it is fairyland psychiatry, yet not totally unrelated to neurotic reality. That is, inductive theory is built from a little truth. We are not a hydraulic cylinder with valves. What has all this to do with believing or not believing in a benevolent God? I recall when, several years ago, I was viscerally deep in accomplished criminal offenders, I saw a gastroenterologist because I had stomach problems from what he said was being over-stressed. I told the doctor I did not need his medicine, because Coca-Cola released the stomach gas. I remember his direct medical counsel: "Yes, you are getting some out, but you are putting more in than you release."

This is analogous to many therapies. There is temporary release, but the soul of man is not totally free of the emotional virus. Even lesser stress can return the wounded caregiver to the disabling trauma and Dr. Sidney Freedman must be once again called.

About a year ago *Psychology Today* carried an article about ten of the "sacred cows" of therapy that went south. The "hydraulic theory," as I used to call it, was among the ten. So from where do we search for help? In a one-page article two decades ago, I wrote:

> *"Since no man knows God perfectly, so no man knows exactly what it means to have been created in the image and likeness of God. The devout go beyond evolutionary theory to declare that we are spirit and intellect, or mind. Soul is a prerequisite of destiny, and mind is the prerequisite of rational problem solving. What about psychology, the science of mind and behavior? I believe counselors have a duty under God to study psychology. Deliberate and relentless care must be taken to avoid a 'Weltanschauung' (World-and-Life view) that would agree with Freud's statement that 'men of good will can erect the house of science only on the ruins of religion.' God has not left us without direction in determining how the devout deal with psychology. In 2 Chr. 16:12, we find Asa, King of Judah,*

faced with a similar problem. 'Though his disease was severe, even in his illness he did not seek help from the Lord, but only from the physicians.' To work only with psychology, is to go it alone without God."

The next verse in Scripture is one that deeply saddens me. "So Asa rested with his fathers; he died in the forty-first year of his life." (2 Chr. 16:13). Asa broke the Creator/creature equation and went only with man's medical science.

CHAPTER 25

Psychology Books No Flights to God

Psychology, at its best, is a human enterprise. Psychology, at its best, is a mortal being's enterprise. For me to bet my life on psychology is analogous to following the genius of Parmenides and Descartes to an acknowledgment of the existence of mortal being and then stopping abruptly. That is stopping short of Eternal Being.

A couple of years ago, while enmeshed in the donkey stew of training for pastoral care in one of Tucson's finest hospitals, I wrote a short paper entitled, "A Chaplain Delineates Theology and Psychology." It was well-received by unbelievers and believers alike. The most complimentary remarks with thanks came from unbelievers. Here is at least half of this short paper.

1. The epistemology of psychology is human study. The etiology of theology is God.

2. Psychology studies God's creation, that is man. Theology studies the Creator of man and His claims on man.

3. All scientific psychology revealed a faulted creature. Theology alone offers redemption to the faulted creature.

4. Psychology is confined within the first creation, the Genesis story. Theology includes the second, redemptive creation in Christ by way of His sacrifice, not ours.

5. Psychology is mortal, for all men die. Theology is eternal, for God is eternal.

6. Psychology offers the best of human knowledge. Theology is premised in Divine revelation.

7. Psychological care giving should offer love, peace, patience, kindness, goodness, faithfulness, and gentleness. In theology, "love, joy, peace, patience, kindness, goodness, faithfulness, gentleness, self-control" are the gifts of the Holy Spirit and are the nature of Christ Himself, therefore eternal (Gal. 5:22, 23). *English Standard Bible.* They are ours for the asking.

8. In psychology, the qualities of #7 are creature-powered. In theology, the gifts of the Spirit are Divinely energized. He, the Holy Spirit, generates in us these Christian qualities.

9. Psychology rejects God because even if He exists, the subject is outside its scope of study. Theology begins its study with God and ends with man's redemption.

10. Psychology focuses on individuality therefore limiting its care giving. Theology's focus is on *(Koimōmos)* fellowship that is established in grace united by the Spirit through the Son to the Father. There are no limits.

11. Individuality dies when the individual's body dies. Theology offers to each individual membership into the body of Christ, which is eternal. It reunites creature with the Creator through redemption.

12. Psychology can communicate by pedagogic technique because it is human in its origin and essence. Theology can only be taught by the power of the Holy Spirit; herein truth becomes efficacious in our lives.

13. Psychology says we have all the answers you will ever need. Theology says knowledge unto salvation is by Divine revelation solely.

14. In psychology, faulted man studies faulted phenomenon by unavoidable faulty method in hope of resolving man's faults. In theology, man studies God who faulted natural man and nature because of sin, and freely offers a solution for man's dilemma.

15. In psychology, you must do obeisance to the dominant culture to be accepted professionally. In theology, your faulted, sinful self is accepted, even unto redemption and sonship of God.

16. In psychology, you can have all it offers that is the best of human wisdom that denies any claim of God, and you can take a paradigmatic approach to care giving that will never make you feel guilty. In theology, you must acknowledge your faulted creatureliness and accept Christ's redemptive program and in care giving really lose the life of the self psychology would evolve for you. "Whoever finds his life will lose it, and whoever loses his life for my sake will find it" (Matt. 10:39 ESV). It's a joyous approach to caregiving.

For psychology to book you flights to God would be to prostitute its own science and bring its house down on its head. Sigmund Freud boasted that psychology would build a house of science on the ashes of religion. I commend him for distinguishing the difference between the "being" of Parmenides and the "becoming" of Heraclitus. But he forgot that you cannot have change or motion without Being.

Stories are told of Freud when, at private parties, the subject of death had to be avoided, lest he would faint and hit the floor. Is it possible that in his philosophy of denying Ultimate Being, he never felt emotionally secure? As I have mentioned before, mortality will not be denied a hearing in life's court, surely not in my mortal life.

God is truly not an issue of psychology but it is up to the psychologists who rush outside their science to explain their motives. I challenge any psychologist to break their motivational silence and show me the praxeological justification for fence-jumping. For most of you who work diligently on your side of the scientific fence to alleviate the frustration of the human condition, I commend you. I feel the weight of the task you have undertaken.

On the subject of psychology, I am more often misunderstood than not. I am as serious a student of psychology as I am a serious student of finite human life. My obtrusiveness is sensed in others because I have no confidence in either of the above subjects to effect eternal peace with God.

CHAPTER 26

Psychology Books No Flights to God II

Psychology, by its own presuppositions about God, must of necessity travel the road of evolution. This, by itself, satisfies my offense with the science.

I was a devout Freudian when I accepted a position with the Superior Court of Arizona. I was assigned to capital offenses, those crimes for which capital punishment was prescribed in law. In five of my first eight murder cases, the persons were under psychotherapy at the time the offenses were committed. To view these figures as cause-and-effect is naïve; however, the Hippocratic Oath avowing "do no harm" appears frustrated. I then turned, as my mother called it, to old-country psychology and away from American psychology. Non-American psychologists (there are some exceptions) distinguish between human and animal subject matter. They also permit ideology a place in their psychology. Continental scholars are sensitive so as not to be guilty of reification by changing praxis to process. Psychology is never so tragic as when it loses sight of man as distinct being.

What do continental psychologists and philosophers mean when they accuse us of reification by way of turning praxis into process? Simply expressed, it is an attempt to try to change human action into impersonal activity. Praxis has no truly adequate English translation. Psychologist David Ingleby wrote, "While process describes the behavior of inanimate objects, accounted for wholly by causes, praxis is the medium of the specifically human; it implies behavior which is purposive and accountable for only in terms of its meaningfulness." David Ingleby, *Ideology and the Human Sciences, The Human Context*, Vol. II, No. 2, July 1970.[11] How long has it been since you witnessed a psychologist free himself from his "evolutionistic" premises and speak to you as a unique creation of God? Psychologists will give you permission to be whatever accommodates their science. Psychology is nothing more than humanism that has gone to college and learned a manageable methodology in hopes of gaining public respect.

Again, I wish to remind my readers that I do not view experience as truth, but something analogous to truth that has some capacity, like other evidence, to point to or touch truth when sound rationality is applied.

What has psychology got to do with unbelief and or belief in God? It masquerades as ultimate truth, but it is the product of mortal beings, not Eternal Being. It may not produce the results you had hoped for seeing its acceptance in our culture and its high position in academic institutes.

There was a psychologist in London by the name of Hans Jurgan Eysenck, who was a major contributor to scientific psychology. He did very extensive research on the effects of psychotherapy. The research paper appears in the *International Journal of Psychiatry*, Vol. 1, January 1965.

> *"This research showed that by the end of two years, 67% of the patients improved, treated or not; by the end of five years, 95% improved, treated or not. 'Neurotic patients treated by means of psychotherapeutic procedure, based on learning theory, improved significantly more quickly than do patients treated by means of psychoanalytic or electic psychotherapy or not treated by psychotherapy."*[12]

No, it is not a recent research study, but it set the scientific guidelines for studies that were to follow. It is hard to improve on those minimal results. I count 213 references to worldwide scholars published in the *International Journal of Psychiatry*. Dr. Eysenck came to my attention when, in his book, *Crime and Personality*, I read, "Man is the most deadly animal which has ever lived in this world, yet we fail to recognize it." Psychology is hardly worth worshiping as a substitute for faith in a sole Eternal Being.

I would share just one more quote from Dr. David Ingleby that you can compare image and likeness of God to what psychology offers you:

> *"The psychiatrist never says, 'You do not hate;' instead, he says, 'Your aggression is a symptom.' This response offers the patient a kind of recognition of which he is probably in great need: by appearing to account for his behavior and experience, it holds out for him a kind of non-identity. Thus eagerly accepted, this identity soon reveals itself as non-identity; the patient finds himself with a self-concept in which his deviance is portrayed as non-human, malignant process, so that unless he abandons his former self—literally loses his mind—he will be assigned to perpetual mortification."*[13]

What about integrating the two sciences, theology and psychology? Sincere and devoted friends tell me I miss the power of major academic trends by my unyielding stand. I do believe in the integration of the sciences, but stop short and abruptly when it comes to theology.

If theology is revealed, not discovered, and I believe it is, I would be betraying scientific methodology integrating these two. Integration never improves theology because it prostitutes the Creator/creature equation. Ministers, do I have your ears?

CHAPTER 27
Escape into Acknowledgment

"Acknowledgment, the act of confession: approving: as in the acknowledgment of God." *American Dictionary of the English Language*, Noah Webster, 1828. Solely on the human plane, I have long wished that someone would ask me for just one word that they can understand that separates believers from unbelievers. To date, no one has asked me. When they do, I will respond with the word "acknowledgment," as I now will attempt to define it for you, the readers.

Acknowledgment is a big word in the Bible, in both the Old and New Testaments:

> *"Therefore know this day, and consider it in your heart, that the Lord Himself is God in heaven above and on the earth beneath; there is no other. You shall therefore keep His statutes and His commandments which I command you today, that it may go well with you and with your children after you, and that you may prolong your days in the land which the Lord your God is giving you for all time." (Deut. 4:39–40)*

> *"Acknowledge is a powerful term. It has deep moral implications when directed inward and deep religious significance when*

applied to one's relationship with God. When we grasp what it means to acknowledge God and to acknowledge our sins, we sense much more fully the unique commitment to which faith calls us." Lawrence O. Richards, Expository Dictionary of Bible Words[14]

I have not mentioned it earlier in the book, but whenever we speak of any relationship, we are immediately immersed in a moral sphere where the Lordship of God determines moral standards and conduct. When we take a wife and exchange marriage vows, those vows are replete with the moral conditions of a marriage covenant. There is hardly anything else to the marriage vows. The acknowledgment of a relationship with God is not as frightening as it seems at first blush. God is very predictable and does not flip-flop, as is characteristic of lesser beings. He is the One taking a chance on any relationship with us. This is not a vis-à-vis covenant.

"Trust in the Lord with all your heart, and lean not on your own understanding; in all your ways acknowledge Him, and He shall direct your paths. Do not be wise in your own eyes; fear the Lord and depart from evil." (Prov. 3:5-7, The Proverbs of Solomon, son of David)

Acknowledgment clearly requires a switch in loyalties and confidence from our self to God. Lordship is always singular. We must remember that it is possible to have knowledge and not to acknowledge. Acknowledgment of God requires a good knowledge of God. It is very easy to find unbelievers with only a vague knowledge of God. We have all been reluctant to learn deep truths about God for fear we would have to treat Him with utmost respect and seriousness. It is quite natural to treat ourselves with utmost seriousness. The self naturally ascends to the throne of lordship. *Webster's Dictionary* also used the word "confession." Confession is from the Greek word *homologeō*, which means "to say the same" thing God said about life and morals. Is God neutral or passive in all this? Not a chance under heaven. Let us hear David on the subject:

> *"When I consider Your heavens, the work of Your fingers, the moon and the stars, which You have ordained, what is man that You are mindful of him, and the son of man that You visit him? For You have made him a little lower than the angels, and You have crowned him with glory and honor. You have made him to have dominion over the works of Your hands; You have put all things under his feet." (Ps. 8:3-6)*

When it came to the New Testament and a New Covenant, a creation in Christ's blood, God binds Himself to those who acknowledge His only Son. "If anyone acknowledges that Jesus is the Son of God, God lives in him and he in God" (1 John 4:15, NIV). Acknowledgment is a failsafe zone, because God became the Guarantor of the new relationship (Heb. 7:22, NIV). Remembering He is eternal, His word is as sure as His life. "Truths" in psychology change for man is mortal and death is change. Change to the eternal soul is like terminal cancer.

CHAPTER 28
Not All Are Volunteers

"Many are the plans in the mind of a man, but it is the purpose of the Lord that will stand." (Prov. 19:21 ESV)

I have been arguing for a respectful academic level of rationality as an aid in discovering Eternal Being and/or God. Both are the same. What I am saying poorly is that I cannot, while writing principally to unbelievers, offer a totally comfortable rationale for the subject of this chapter, beyond what is found in Sacred Scripture and in the testimony of honorable men. The testimony of honorable men had better count for something. Honorable men rise above the mere definition of human beings.

The subject, stated perhaps too simply, is that some men become believers in the Christ of God who never volunteered, or if they did, were unaware it happened. I am not going to argue their stories. I am just going to quote them briefly.

The first is Noah Webster, 1758-1843. His credentials are impressive. I have already quoted his dictionary of 1828. He defines voluntary "as acting by choice without being influenced by another." In the introduction to *The American Dictionary of the English Language,* I found these quotes. He tells of a respectable revival held in New Haven, which his family was attending. He was concerned that an approach to religion be rational and not misled by the danger of passion or fanaticism. He tells:

"I did not forbid [his family] but rather discouraged their attendance on conferences…'These impressions I attempted to remove by reasoning with myself and endeavoring to quiet my mind by a persuasion that my opposition to my family and the awakening was not a real opposition to rational religion but to enthusiasm or false religion. I continued some weeks in this situation, utterly unable to quiet my own mind and without resorting to the only source of peace and consolation. The impressions, however, grew stronger till at length I could not pursue my studies without frequent interruptions. My mind was suddenly arrested, without any previous circumstance of the time to draw it to this subject and, as it were, fastened to the awakening and upon my own conduct. I closed my books, yielded to the influence which could not be resisted or mistaken, and was led by a spontaneous impulse to repentance, prayer, and entire submission and surrender of myself to my Maker and Redeemer. My submission appeared to be cheerful, and was soon followed by that peace of mind which the world can neither give nor take away.

'This, my dear friend, is a short but faithful narration of facts. That these impressions were not the effect of any of my own passions nor of enthusiasm is to me evident, for I was in complete possession of all my rational powers, and that the influence was supernatural is evident from this circumstance; it was not only independent of all volition but opposed to it. "[15]

May I suggest that Sovereignty ruled this Creator/creature equation? Sovereignty cannot but rule, yet He is incredibly sensitive to the creature being.

The next person I have chosen was the eminent scholar C.S. Lewis who, just before his death, held the chair of Medieval and Renaissance English Literature at Cambridge. The quote is from his book *Surprised by Joy*. As with Webster, I would not presume to elaborate on his words.

> *"You must picture me alone in that room in Magdalen, night after night, feeling, whenever my mind lifted even for a second from my work, the steady, unrelenting approach of Him whom I so earnestly desired not to meet. That which I greatly feared had at last come upon me. In the Trinity Term of 1929 I gave in, and admitted that God was God, and knelt and prayed: perhaps, that night, the most dejected and reluctant convert in all England. I did not then see what is now the most shining and obvious thing; the Divine humility which will accept a convert even on such terms. The Prodigal Son at least walked home on his own feet. But who can duly adore that Love which will open the high gates to a prodigal who is brought in kicking, struggling, resentful, and darting his eyes in every direction for a chance to escape? The words* compelle intrare, *compel them to come in, have been so abused by wicked men that we shudder at them; but, properly understood, they plumb the depth of the Divine mercy. The hardness of God is kinder than the softness of men, and His compulsion is our liberation."*[16]

My third selection is Saul of Tarsus, who was to become the Apostle Paul. The quote is a portion of Paul's testimony before King Agrippa following his arrest and is recorded in the New

Testament, the Book of Acts, chapter 26:9-19. You will find Acts right after the four Gospels.

> *"Indeed, I myself thought I must do many things contrary to the name of Jesus of Nazareth. This I also did in Jerusalem, and many of the saints I shut up in prison, having received authority from the chief priests; and when they were put to death, I cast my vote against them. And I punished them often in every synagogue and compelled them to blaspheme, and being exceedingly enraged against them, I persecuted them even to foreign cities. While thus occupied, as I journeyed to Damascus with authority and commission from the chief priests, at midday, O king, along the road I saw a light from heaven, brighter than the sun, shining around me and those who journeyed with me. And when we all had fallen to the ground, I heard a voice speaking to me and saying in the Hebrew language, 'Saul, Saul, why are you persecuting Me? It is hard for you to kick against the goads.' So I said, 'Who are You, Lord?' And He said, 'I am Jesus, whom you are persecuting. But rise and stand on your feet; for I have appeared to you for this purpose, to make you a minister and a witness both of the things which you have seen and of the things which I will yet reveal to you. I will deliver you from the Jewish people, as well as from the Gentiles, to whom I now send you, to open their eyes, in order to turn them from darkness to light, and from the power of Satan to God, that they may receive forgiveness of sins and an inheritance among those who are sanctified by faith in Me.' Therefore, King Agrippa, I was not disobedient to the heavenly vision."*

Paul's conversion was not an adjustment. It was a 180-degree turn regarding Jesus, who is the Messiah.

If I am conscious as to why I put this chapter together, it is to show by three very special and academically credible witnesses that God is sovereign over the affairs of men, including their eternal salvation. Were you a trial lawyer, how would you feel if on your witness list appeared Noah Webster, C.S. Lewis, and the Apostle Paul? Think about it. A scholar from America, one from England, and a devout Jew from the Middle East. God, in supreme Sovereignty, chose three great witnesses from among us. They were not passive in terms of vital beings, yet none initiated anything of personal mind, heart, or willfulness.

I am caused to introduce a concept from philosophy and theology. It is the concept of transcendence. When confronting criminal offenders, I have asked, "Did your self-monitoring system blow a fuse?" A blank face often meant that no such monitoring system was involved or was caused to be evolved. Man can transcend his action at one and the same time that acts are in motion. So we have the concept of "up and over." However, when trying to describe God, the above illustration is too anthropomorphic. Experiencing God is greater than just being "up and over."

> *"Soren Kierkegaard maintained that there is an 'infinite qualitative difference' between humans and God, and that humans, due to their sinful nature, are tempted to domesticate God to make God serve them. Like Calvin, however, Kierkegaard offers an account of God's 'accommodation' to finitude by condescending to our level. In this respect, the incarnation is taken as the paradigm of God's 'condescension,' bridging the gap between transcendence and immanence."* 101 Key Terms in Philosophy and Their Importance to Theology,[17] Kelly James Clark, Richard Lints, James K.A. Smith

What I am attempting to say a bit more simply is that while God is both transcendent and accommodating in Christ, He alone is sovereign and can transcend the Redeemer/redeemed equation I so often write about. All three men in this chapter came to acknowledgment after God dramatically moved first and effectively unto salvation.

> *"Augustine held that God is like a vast ocean: even the unlearned can paddle about in the shallows and the trained theologian can swim out a bit farther; but both are of such limited ability that they would be swallowed up in the depths."*[18] *(ibid, p. 96)*

God said to Moses, "I will be gracious to whom I will be gracious, and I will have compassion on whom I will have compassion." (Ex. 33:19)

CHAPTER 29
Moving in for a Closer Look

In the last chapter, I quoted three great witnesses from history whom, if I were a trial lawyer, I would entreat to be on my witness list. If I were alive then, I would have sought their counsel. Now I would entreat the reader to allow me to posit a question: What if these three men, Noah Webster, C.S. Lewis, and the Apostle Paul, came up with a solely self-determined definition of God for each witness? Would their conversion, sinner to redeemed, have been as they themselves described? Their conversions were from lost to found, from nihilism to the presence of Eternal Being, and from a mortal's death to eternal life.

Let's return to a very mundane plane. I cannot avoid the advertising on television of eHarmony.com. They will find you a soul mate as near to yourself as psychology can measure. Can you imagine on your wedding night jumping into bed with yourself, with the sole exception of only another's body form?

This is a serious book, so I will not push my analogy to its next logical step. Clearly, they are selling self-love, which came so naturally to us all without the help of commercial brokers. The jewel of love is posited in the other. In the context of this book, the jewel of love is posited in The Other. I warned you that the illustration was mundane. If God left us to ourselves, our feet would leave prints in the desert sand from conception to the grave, where we would leave a body print. I did truly mean conception, since after birth, all lasting prints are body prints, inasmuch as some of us have already accepted that "to dust you shall return." Such is the harsh nature of mortal reality.

None of us, before our conversion, could have been able to define God. As on eHarmony.com, we will only define another in kind, even though we give him the name God. Such is the prison sentence of self-love. This is why inordinate self-love does not rise to the definition of love in Scripture.

If we do not love the God who is self-defined, we do not love God at all. In our Creator/creature equation, the creature cannot define God. Start with loving your neighbor for whom you can define love fairly well.

> *"Then one of them, a lawyer, asked Him a question, testing Him, and saying, 'Teacher, which is the great commandment in the law?' Jesus said to him, 'You shall love the Lord your God with all your heart, with all your soul, and with all your mind. This is the first and great commandment. And the second is like it: You shall love your neighbor as yourself. On these two commandments hang all the Law and the Prophets.'" (Matt 22:35–40)*

If you get past the first half of the great commandment, you would have diminished your inflated self-image to where loving your neighbor is a cakewalk. Your self-love is now adjusted to creature size.

When Moses was told that God's name was "I AM WHO I AM" (Ex. 3:14), the meaning more than states a simple identity. It conveys something of the very essence of His Eternal Being. It is as if God bets His reputation and character on His name. While I AM means self-existing Eternal Being, it also means self-identifying. It cannot mean other than self-naming, and this without exception or help by any creature being or one thousand.

The third commandment of the Big Ten denies us misuse of God's name. This commandment goes far beyond swearing. I am certain it also includes the use of euphemism even when said respectfully as in "the man upstairs" since these are diminishing synthetic terms. We do not possess the intellect to comprehend "I AM WHO I AM." Reverence of God's name is always becoming the lesser being. It becomes the reverent created being. In the next chapter, we will move in closer.

CHAPTER 30
Moving in Still Closer

I have mentioned earlier in the book how disquieting it is for me to even think of trying to prove God's existence from created beings of created stuff. I sense something like nausea in my spiritual being. Since the Creator of Life is singular and lesser beings cannot create life, I cannot make a truly analogous comparison.

What if, in the realm of pure imagination, you had the capacity to create dependent life in likeness and this lesser life continued *ad nauseam*, trying for literally centuries upon centuries to decide simply if you had existence? Would not your sense of benevolence be troubled, even taxed to its limits? Now to study an artist's works so as to glean something about the artist is a different subject matter. Still, just no one viewing true art asks if there is an artist.

The sole Creator of all life and matter took one more giant step to become known to us. He left a written record where at times He even dictated verbatim truths about Himself like "I AM WHO I AM" or "thou shall call His name Jesus." For certain, He did not send us to the moon and other planets to search for the origin of the cosmos or even for human life for that matter.

I find nowhere in Scripture where we have any responsibility to entertain God with humor. If we were out there looking for some superior being with which to consult, I would feel a bit more comfortable. If we cannot create genuine life from inanimate material, why are we looking for such inanimate materials that will prove our origin of life? Has our hatred of the Creator grown so strong that we hope we find evidence for life from non-life materials? From nothing comes nothing. God made Adam from ground, but He was true God. We can always power up our imagination with the fuel of conjecture, publish the article and be assured to persuade a good number of gullible readers.

The Bible spoke before the age of modern science about what could be known about God from nature. It really says what must be known to avoid conviction. It is not an opinion.

> *"For the wrath of God is revealed from heaven against all ungodliness and unrighteousness of men, who suppress the truth in unrighteousness, because what may be known of God is manifest in them, for God has shown it to them. For since the creation of the world His invisible attributes are clearly seen, being understood by the things that are made, even His eternal power and Godhead, so that they are without excuse."* *(Rom. 1:18-20)*

"The invisible attributes" may be a little tricky. Webster, in his original dictionary, defines attribute as "to give as due; to yield as an act of mind; as, to attribute to God all the glory of redemption." The original Greek has some true irony, as it would be "his unseeable qualities ... are clearly seen."

What St. Paul is telling us is that in viewing and experiencing nature, we should, by the native power of our rationality, attribute eternal power and never-failing omnipotence to God. This was possible before man invented the telescope and the microscope. With today's science, the evidence in nature is trumpeted still more loudly. Order alone makes science possible. Science did not put order out there.

If we deny God, nature by itself will bring in a jury verdict of guilty and the Judge of the whole universe will pronounce us guilty. Again, that is what Paul is saying. I do not find a hint in Scripture that would allow the lesser being to avoid prosecution by the denial of available evidence.

In the next chapter, I want us to view what Scripture directly says about God, that is, what can we know and what must we acknowledge.

CHAPTER 31
Defining God by His Word

We all have our point of sacred reference. At our worst, it is in the egotistical self, and at our best, it is in God. Every attempt to define God should be a sacred task.

The old Hebrew scribes would go through twenty-four-hour purification, cut a new quill, and make just a single letter, neither spelling out nor pronouncing the holy name of Yahweh.

The best definition of God I know anything about comes to us from the Westminster Assembly, in the form of the Larger Catechism that was completed April 14, 1648. Assembly members were forbidden to argue any issue of doctrinal meaning from human philosophy, ecclesiastical authority, or ecclesiastical reputation. The Bible was the sole reference for acceptance or rejection of doctrine. It was *scriptura solo* all the way.

Article II "of God and the Holy Trinity" is too long, and its older English words are not suitable for my purpose and intent for this short book. That which follows is extractions:

- God's perfection is seen in His absolute Being.
- God's will is most righteous.
- God's counsel is most wise.
- God is most loving beyond our comprehension.

- God is always and everywhere truth.
- God is forgiving, gracious, and long-suffering.
- God is absolute holiness and cannot tolerate sin in His presence.
- God rewards all who diligently seek Him,
- God's judgments are terrible yet absolutely just.
- God does not need one or all of us lesser beings. We need Him,
- God, unlike us lesser beings, is adorned by glory and honor.
- God is the origin of all beings and sustains all beings.
- God has dominion over all beings.
- God sees all things even the invisible passions of our heart.
- God requires worship, service, and obedience, all of which He is pleased to require of us all.

I need to pause and, with the force of humility, blow the crud out of the fissures of my cerebral cortex before I continue. I would feel more comfortable just now had I gone through a time of purification, dressed in sackcloth and put ashes in my hair. I share the confession of David: "Behold, I was brought forth in iniquity, and in sin my mother conceived me" (Ps. 51:5). Let us continue.

- God is invisible spirit yet no less Eternal Being.
- God's knowledge of all things is without limitation.
- God is not fully comprehensible to lesser beings.
- God has presence anywhere and everywhere in the universe at one and the same time.
- God is Eternal and has no beginning or end.
- God's power knows no measure, no limitations.
- God is most free because He is self-existent and dependent on no one and nothing outside Himself.
- God is the creator of all things.
- God is active in all creation, yet not identified with or by creation, including man. He is complete without creation.

- God creates no other gods, else He would not be God.
- God has not made His first mistake ever, even with sinners like me. The debit side of the ledger is all mine.
- God is not out to get us, but if you chose to run, you will not escape.
- God can regenerate our human nature without killing our bodies or our spirits. We cannot love God without an inner-nature regeneration. Call it the heart.
- God is One yet Triune and can take counsel within Himself (Gen. 1:26). Such counsel brought us lesser beings into existence.
- God's word is His bond, His eternal covenant with us. There will be no future that is not determined by God. God entertains no surprises.

This list is shamefully lacking, but it is quite enough for redemptive acknowledgment. There is wisdom in giving it deep and serious consideration, because it is what God said about Himself in His writings to us called the Holy Bible.

Amen. Webster defines "amen" as "it is so; so be it." Amen and Amen.

Question One of the Shorter Catechism appeals to me as a postscript following the sobering reality of attempting to define God. We do understand question one:

"Q. 1. What is the chief and highest end of man?

A. Man's chief and highest end is to glorify God, and fully to enjoy him forever."

Many believers tell me they never formulated a concept of God in their mind. One even told me that not knowing whom you believe in does not depart from sound logic, especially as it relates to my oft-quoted Creator/creature equation.

CHAPTER 32
God Buys Used Guilt

Guilt is our most convicting witness to us that we are not God. There is more true truth in the foregoing sentence, to borrow an expression from the late Dr. Francis A. Schaeffer, than in everything the God-hating Sigmund Freud has written on guilt.

The youngest man ever to graduate from the University of Arizona Law College shouted a retort at me that I was failing to consider that Freud gave us a language to talk about the problem of people. What Freud never gave us was a meaningful language to talk about and approach the problem of guilt in mental illness as guilt relates to the Creator/creature equation.

The burning embers of Freud's unproven and improvable theory remain and are a stench in the nostrils of caring beings. Why his theory continues to be published carries a sense of esoteric mystery. I have often thought that the big-brained animal with one or more degrees from college is challenged just to follow him through the mystical mazes he evolved about the guilt-ridden personality.

I just finished reading some such definition in the elitist *Dictionary of Pastoral Care and Counseling,* Rodney O. Hunter, general editor. The author writes that the modern approach to the psychodynamics of guilt will usually involve three theories. "These are the psychoanalytic, cognitive-learning, and behavioral theories."[19]

For the purposes of brevity, Mr. Hunter chose the psychoanalytic explanation of the guilt process. No jury of academicians has ever found Freud guilty of brevity after many trials on both sides of the Atlantic Ocean. The two theories that the author of the definition on guilt chose to set aside without further comment are cognitive-learning and behavioral theories. Both of these can be approached with cognition. This simply means they can be studied by well-established scientific methods that can be perceived and known.

Freud's theory of personal and moral development casts us solely on our faith in the opinion and academic reputation of the author. Freud denies us, by the nature of his theory, a rational and scientific examination of what he promulgates. If you appreciate irony, it was Freud who said, "Psychiatry shall build a house of science on the ashes of religion."

Why do we continue to quote Freud as having something substantial to say about guilt? Is it blind academic inertia or is our hatred of God so impregnated in our faulted natures that we are content to worship at the altar of lesser demons? The author of the definition of guilt gets a single sentence right if judged in the context of traditional Reformation Theology (soteriology). "We are liberated from alienation and the power of sin and guilt when we accept and live in the context of God's Love." Dr. Francis A. Schaeffer gave us the expression "true truth." I like the expression "simple profundity," as it is applicable to the last quote. Psychoanalytic theory and psychology will cloud the true truth. The true truth is comprehended in simplicity, not in profundity; it is God's love that is profound, hence you have simple profundity.

I do not minimize guilt. I share the insight with psychology that it is gravel in the gears of the psyche. No one is excluded, not even the psychopath, for he feels the guilt of alienation. If there were no immortal life with God for a lesser being without faith in Christ and only life in the flesh, belief in God would be a small price to pay to "sell" Him our guilt.

Freud developed a theory of personality formation that accommodates guilt as a factor in structure and wholesome balance between id, ego, and superego. Psychotherapy is intended to restore balance. For me, Freud never answered the question of how the soul expiates itself of guilt by well-reasoned conscience or with God. Most of you readers know that if Freud could have, he would have had all guilt charged to God. Man's failure in moral conduct leads to guilt. God, on the other hand, is the only one who will buy it by simple confession. It is just as easy as confessing love to our best girl. Confession is exposing the soul to someone. In confession to God, He will never cross-reference you.

I never got to the chapter title, but I will defend the title in the next chapter.

CHAPTER 33
God Buys Used Guilt, II

If we wear guilt five minutes, it is used guilt and it is ours personally. While all the behavioral sciences are stuck in the quicksand of subjective guilt, the believer in God and His Redemptive Christ hold out a complete acquittal from objective guilt and its necessary accompanying subjective guilt. The two are inseparable without special help from God, known as grace.

Christianity has no philosophical or psychological theory about subjective guilt. Christianity has only a theological theory. Its purpose and expressed goal, by the power of God's Spirit, is to get rid of or reduce to remission the negative subjective feeling in the personality of believers. Even tolerating guilt, except as a corrective compass between right and wrong, is held up as real sin in the Christian life (2 Cor. 7:8-10).

Whoever tells you that you can forgive yourself independent of God, in Christ, is full of ka-ka *(A Dictionary of Slang)*. It simply does not get the human waste (sin) out of the being of man, since all sin, without exception, is against a Holy God. Do not be shocked with my language. You used the word with babies. It is quite descriptive.

While guilt is always a small remnant fact in the experience of believing Christians because we are never as holy as commanded, let no one doubt that total remission of sin, and its subjective counterpart guilt, is not always and everywhere the standard of normalcy. Becoming guilt-free, both objective and subjective, is the declared goal for a normal daily walk in this secular world, not just the walk to church or a vacation to a monastery.

Secular psychology completely ignores objective guilt with God. Many, even most, pastoral-care counselors are reading Scripture with corrective glasses and changing to opaque glasses when they read Sigmund Freud and his enduring converts. In Scripture, guilt is both a fact and a feeling. It is solely God who forgives the sin that makes the uncomfortable feeling. The term "negative feeling" is all but absent in the New Testament. Objective guilt is only translated into feeling words twice in the New International Version. You cannot keep God out of objective or subjective guilt. "Against You, You only, have I sinned. And done this all in Your sight ..." (Ps. 5:4). There are no saints born into the human race in God's sight. "For all have sinned and fall short of the glory of God" (Rom. 3:23). Birth into the human race is the starting line for sin in the human personality. Yes, sin is an act, but worse than the act of sin is a condition in the soul of everyone. When a pastoral-care person finds guilt in a care receiver, he has made no noteworthy discovery. We have subjective—yes, objective also—guilt by what we are first, then by what we do.

Remittance is by confession to the offended Eternal Being, then to lesser offended beings. The biting logic is only believers can truly confess acts to the all-Holy God. The unbeliever must first confess a heart problem that generates willful sin, since it has meaning to the self.

Therefore, sin—the forerunner of guilt—always appears in Scripture. Then guilt appears as having three distinct parts: the act that makes guilt, the condition of guilt in all unbelievers, and the appropriate punishment for the act. Because all sins are offenses against God, guilt can only be understood by relating it to God.

Some counselors—most secular counselors—take God out of the equation, so as not to make the client feel negative feelings still more intensely. I feel like shouting directions at them, "Have you ever truly understood God's willing forgiveness as painless medication?" Confession is total remission objectively and subjectively for guilt.

In the next chapter, I will do verbal heart surgery on the glorious Gospel of Christ. Before psychology came into view, God hated secular guilt. St. Paul called it a killer. He also called godly guilt that leads to repentance a life-giver (2 Cor. 7:8-10). You do not have to go to a psychiatrist, a medical doctor for a prescription, surely not to an amoral secular counselor, not even to the local bar for some good stiff drinks. Just go in humility to the only absolutely Holy Being you have ever heard of and repent.

What have you been doing about your guilt? Many unbelievers avoid God in an attempt to not deal with guilt. That is why I included the subject of guilt in this book.

CHAPTER 34

Born Again, Science or Theology?

"There was a man of the Pharisees named Nicodemus, a ruler of the Jews. This man came to Jesus by night and said to Him, 'Rabbi, we know that You are a teacher come from God; for no one can do these signs that You do unless God is with him.' Jesus answered and said to him, 'Most assuredly, I say to you, unless one is born again, he cannot see the kingdom of God.' Nicodemus said to Him, 'How can a man be born when he is old? Can he enter a second time into his mother's womb and be born?' Jesus answered; 'Most assuredly, I say to you, unless one is born of water and the Spirit, he cannot enter the kingdom of God. That which is born of the flesh is flesh, and that which is born of the Spirit is spirit. Do not marvel that I said to you, You must be born again.'" (John 3:1-7)

Dr. William D. Phillips is a 1997 recipient of the Nobel Prize in Physics. Writing in June 2006 *Science and Theology News*, he says:

"Just as science cannot prove the existence of God, I insist just as firmly that science cannot disprove the existence of God because it's not a scientific issue."[20]

Dr. Phillips encourages his readers to ask the right question of the right scientific discipline. It is as if Nicodemus had read the article two thousand years before it was written. Nicodemus acknowledged both a natural and a spiritual realm. A few years ago, I wrote the same message with reference to psychiatry and theology. While I got some high academic praise from both believers and unbelievers, no one offered to buy me lunch. Analysis precedes synthesis.

The Bible never suggests that the study of natural scientific causes will give us the answer to Nicodemus's question. Ultimate cause and spiritual rebirth are the subject of theology. I must return to my oft-quoted Creator/creature equation to explain salvation. David wrote: "Salvation belongs to the Lord" (Ps. 3:8). If you depart from the Creator/creature equation, there is no salvation. When it comes to salvation, political correctness is a roadmap to hell itself.

The people who say that God is solely love should write St. Paul and ask if he would consider changing the attributes he wrote about in Romans 1:20 to a singular attribute: love. The outstanding attribute of God is absolute holiness. Holiness may well be God's most elemental character, rather than an attribute. God's holiness can surely kill, because we are so far removed from it by our native nature.

The distinction between Creator and creature cannot be bridged by man, not even by his educated mind. If a man could get a running start and jump over the Great Wall of China, he could not bridge the chasm that separates the sinner from a Holy God. If anyone is to be saved, and I cannot but marvel that God would save anyone, God must condescend as He did in Christ, to touch and identify with us. Paul, writing to Greece's sin-city at Athens says:

> *"Therefore, if anyone is in Christ, he is a new creation; old things have passed away; behold, all things have become new. Now all things are of God, who has reconciled us to Himself through Jesus Christ, and has given us the ministry of reconciliation, that is, that God was in Christ reconciling the world to Himself, not imputing their trespasses to them, and has committed to us the word of reconciliation. Now then, we are ambassadors for Christ, as though God were pleading through us: we implore you on Christ's behalf, be reconciled to God. For He made Him who knew no sin to be sin for us, that we might become the righteousness of God in Him.," (2 Cor. 5:17-21)*

I cannot comprehend that God would make His Holy and only Begotten Son who knew no sin, sin for us that we might be righteous enough to be received by God. Now love was the motivation in God, but the cost was the death of a Holy One. Love does not grant us the right to be a deadhead about God's holiness.

It was unconditional love that came to church in the cloak of psychology. I mean the kind of love that says sin is not really offensive to God because He is love. Christ's coming was sacrificial love of a divine order. Unconditional love that knows no sin is 100 percent foreign to Sacred Scripture, because it is amoral. It is, by its own definition, amoral. "Love rejoices in the truth"; the whole truth about God (1 Cor. 13:6). If one saint or one thousand saints were to give up their lives, it could not save a child, much less a seasoned sinner. God's standard of holiness would not be met. You can receive sacrificial Divine Love if you give up your desire for independence from God, acknowledge your sinful nature, do an 180-degree U-turn, and be received by Christ. You do not receive Him, He receives you willingly and forever, because Christ took your punishment for your sins and my sins. Love was God's motive to pay our debt, not to excuse it. Divine Love cannot excuse sin. Now the new equation would be Redeemer/redeemed.

This is why I say it is dumb, really dumb, to reject such an offer from God since He is source ONE and ONLY. Near the end of his article, Dr. Phillips writes:

> *"I believe that God acts in the universe in really important ways, and that we will never be able to prove scientifically that this is the case."*[21]

Your eternal salvation is not a scientific issue, so do not look for an answer in science. Psychology can help you be politically correct if that be your determined intent. It has a barrel full of euphemisms. It can help you "to pass away" over against "to die." If we just pass away, what is the sense of maintaining cemeteries? I am sorry, but we will find death blunt. You can experience Christ's redemption with transcendent elation. When a smart man sees a good deal, he buys into it.

CHAPTER 35
Close-ordered Faith

From the lips of One Who was Divine Love in the flesh:

> *"Enter by the narrow gate; for wide is the gate and broad is the way that leads to destruction, and there are many who go in by it. Because narrow is the gate and difficult is the way which leads to life, and there are few who find it." (Matt. 7:13)*

May I share with you the passion I feel for many who would come to the Christian faith without a family background or schooling? Faith in God's economy of salvation is not difficult to understand. May I suggest that the answer to the big question, "How may I be saved?" is made difficult by the enormity of human information in writing and of voice? It is when man tries, with his puny cognitive equipment, to ascend to the heavens to bring God down to anthropomorphic size that the difficulty is created. God did come to earth in the form of man, but no man brought or prayed Him down. Christ chose to come and God sent Him. Once more we have divine truth as dualism.

I must tie my own mind with a taut tether to the Creator/creature equation, now the Redeemer/redeemed equation, lest it take flight. When my imagination won't take the bit in its mouth, I force my imagination to think of a world-size swimming pool without Noah's Ark. If we will not control our imaginations, God may make us a flood built for one.

We know God hates unbridled and independent (independent of God, that is) malignant imaginations. God is recorded reflecting on this subject twice, both before and after the big flood (Gen. 6:5, 8:21). May I attempt to help you, the reader, with what at times seems to be an overwhelming amount of information? Enormity is a problem for me also. My readers say I write best when I stop reading books and write with my head, heart, and hand. Festus said to Paul, "Much learning is driving you mad!" (Acts 26:24). At times, my writing may sound like madness.

In dealing with God's salvation for lost humanity, relativism is a sin, but logical analysis is not. If we accept that salvation is solely from God, to the exclusion of total creation, including man, the enormity of the problem is gone. The diamond cutter's work is finished. The exclusivity of God's offer of salvation is absolutely exclusive. In philosophy, we have to deal with which philosopher said what, where, at what time, and in what context. When God said that Abraham believed God and it was credited to him as righteousness (Gen. 15:6), the time, place, and context are hardly relevant. What God said transcends all other behavioral science considerations, and this includes philosophy. Forgive me if I add ego eruption empowered by rebellious abhorrence for and against God. There are only two involved in your eternal salvation. That is not literally true, but it is a starting point. Now guess which of the two is your problem.

You can limit your source of information drastically. Did God say it through His prophets of the Old Testament? Did He speak through the God-man Jesus, who was the Christ? Did He speak through His disciples and apostles in the New Testament? All of the above are historical reality. All of the above are linked to Ultimate Reality.

> *"But God, who is rich in mercy, because of His great love with*
> *which He loved us, even when we were dead in trespasses,*
> *made us alive together with Christ (by grace you have been*

saved), and raised us up together, and made us sit together in the heavenly places in Christ Jesus, that in the ages to come He might show the exceeding riches of His grace in His kindness toward us in Christ Jesus. For by grace you have been saved through faith, and that not of yourselves; it is the gift of God, not of works, lest anyone should boast." (Eph. 2:4-9)

We have to rely on the free gift of God. This free gift is grace, and to rely completely on grace defines faith. Take a rest from your own faulted egotism. In evaluating all human information about God's salvation, "Let God be true but every man a liar," especially if we tear down the Redeemer/ redeemed equation and put forward a lesser gospel (Rom. 3:4).

Love your neighbor, your fellow man, even the bad guys, especially the unbelievers, at least equal to yourself. Give of your means until your needs are equal to theirs or greater, resulting from your altruism. But accept from no man so-called true truths of salvation if his science is solely human and not divine. Do not accept information about salvation from anyone whom you expect will die a natural death if he or she is the sole human resource of that information. No man after Adam's sin, when death became reality, has the necessary credentials to speak of eternal life. Our pending death burns human credentials. The beloved apostle spoke to this subject. There is just nothing new to learn on the subject.

"Beloved, do not believe every spirit, but test the spirits, whether they are of God; because many false prophets have gone out into the world. By this you know the Spirit of God: Every spirit that confesses that Jesus Christ has come in the flesh is of God, and every spirit that does not confess that Jesus Christ has come in the flesh is not of God. And this is the spirit of the Antichrist, which you have heard was coming, and is now already in the world." (1 John 4:1-3)

Finally, close-ordered faith is never considering ourselves worthy of God's gift, that reconciliation, that cost the Only Begotten His life.

The problem with accepting faith is that egoism which, if not checked, leads to egotism, a more overt and annoying kind of egoism expressed in speech and behavior. When ego would mount my soul, I turn to the Prophet Isaiah and read the passage below:

> *"In the year that King Uzziah died I saw the Lord sitting upon a throne, high and lifted up; and the train of his robe filled the temple. Above him stood the seraphim. Each had six wings: with two he covered his face, and with two he covered his feet, and with two he flew. And one called to another and said: 'Holy, holy, holy is the Lord of hosts; the whole earth is full of his glory!' And the foundations of the thresholds shook at the voice of him who called, and the house was filled with smoke. And I said: 'Woe is me! For I am lost; for I am a man of unclean lips, and I dwell in the midst of a people of unclean lips; for my eyes have seen the King, the Lord of hosts!' Then one of the seraphim flew to me, having in his hand a burning coal that he had taken with tongs from the altar. And he touched my mouth and said: 'Behold, this has touched your lips; your guilt is taken away, and your sin atoned for.'" (Is. 6:1-7 ESV).*

CHAPTER 36

The Weighty Question of Worthiness

From the pen of the beloved Apostle John when he was in the Spirit on the Lord's Day:

> *"Then I looked, and I heard the voice of many angels around the throne, the living creatures, and the elders; and the number of them was ten thousand times ten thousand, and thousands of thousands, saying with a loud voice: 'Worthy is the Lamb who was slain to receive power and riches and wisdom, and strength and honor and glory and blessing!' And every creature which is in heaven and on the earth and under the earth and such as are in the sea, and all that are in them, I heard saying: 'Blessing and honor and glory and power be to Him who sits on the throne, and to the Lamb, forever and ever!' Then the four living creatures said, 'Amen!' And the twenty-four elders fell down and worshiped Him who lives forever and ever."*
> *(Rev. 5:11-14)*

How do you answer a patient dying in ICU at the hospital when he asks, "Chaplain, am I worthy enough of God so He will receive me?" I do not answer in this manner, but here is the answer. All of God's credits for worthiness have been already handed out. The barrel is empty. The patient's question is not a good question in context. Worthiness won't get you one inch off the ground toward heaven. As we say in the marketplace, "Man's worthiness won't feed the bulldog." Yet acknowledging Christ's worthiness and having faith in Him and resting your disquieted soul in Christ will most assuredly get you in. You can, by faith, be received in Christ's worthiness. That's what is so very marvelous about the gospel. Consider this: The offer is a Divine One.

The problem of unworthiness is a terrible subjective experience for many people I see, else I would not write on the subject. It is a problem for seekers or people who desire to be seekers after God. We all hold a Divine invitation to come … that is, get moving.

Guilt and a sense of unworthiness are closely allied subjective experiences. Conscience, especially as the Greeks wrote of it in their literature, is also very closely related. A bad conscience often appears in Greek literature. Conscience can travel backward in our experience, and it is good at focusing in on our past failures. It is a discomforter, but it never clears up the problem of sin with God.

I have met people who believe that conscience is the true God in them and an infallible guide to worthiness before God. The Bible knows of no such infallible conscience. It is not even infallible in strength. If you are an unbeliever and habitually ignore your conscience, it will hardly talk back at you. St. Paul spoke of this to Titus.

> "To the pure, all things are pure, but to those who are defiled and unbelieving nothing is pure; but even their mind and conscience are defiled." (Titus 1:15)

It is hard to feel worthiness before God if your moral watchdog is always barking at you. In context, Jiminy Cricket was wrong when he said,

"Always let your conscience be your guide." The conscience is also part of man's nature faulted by sin. Christ's redemptive work in salvation is not just effective in heavenly places, nor just in places of power on earth, for it reaches into your subjective and cleanses the conscience.

> *"How much more shall the blood of Christ, who through the eternal Spirit offered Himself without spot to God, cleanse your conscience from dead works to serve the living God?" (Heb. 9:14)*

When the conscience is cleansed, the watchdog sleeps. Both its eyes are closed.

If we try to make ourselves subjectively feel worthy before God, whose standards are beyond rational comprehension, we run the risk of going crazy. Any and every criterion we set up, the harder you work at it, the sooner you arrive at crazy. Setting a standard before coming to Christ is foolishness, simply because we are not the one doing the receiving. I beg of you, read the last sentence one more time slowly, and with your God-given cognitive power. Bluntly stated, get out of your way to eternal life.

Salvation is not offered by God as quid pro quo—something for something else. Grace asks nothing but it comes to those who acknowledge their needs. The giant of Old Testament prophets, Isaiah, records God's invitation:

> *"'Come now, and let us reason together,' says the Lord, 'though your sins are like scarlet, they shall be as white as snow; though they are red like crimson, they shall be as wool.'" (Isa. 1:18)*

The focus is on rationality, not worthiness. There is no hint of the necessity of worthiness. Isaiah sets in historical time his meeting with God. When we see God, we have our first real look at ourselves. The self is frozen in place.

CHAPTER 37

Fear: Some Gentle Reality Orientation

"If the fear seems seriously exaggerated—either too great or too little for the actual threat—it may also be helpful and wise, in addition to remaining alert for pathological features, to provide some gentle reality orientation by reviewing the circumstances, distinguishing fact from fearful fantasy or speculation, and helping the person or persons become appropriately aware of the strengths and resources available to them."

The sentence quoted above is from the 1452-page *The Dictionary of Pastoral Care and Counseling*. Rodney J. Hunter, General Editor.[22]

I have never met a human being who has never experienced fear. It is an emotion strong enough to have you unhitch your horse, get into the saddle, and get out of Dodge. Leaving Dodge usually involves avoiding the law or one or more frightening persons. It is usually a person-to-person fear.

Allow me to complicate the problem by returning to our equation of Creator/creature. What if immediately we see that the beings are not equal and flight may not be rational? King David was quite aware of this and acknowledges it in a positive, not a negative, way in Psalm 139. Still, reality always remains reality.

> *"You have hedged me behind and before, and laid Your hand upon me. Such knowledge is too wonderful for me; it is high, I cannot attain it. Where can I go from Your Spirit? Or where can I flee from Your presence? If I ascend into heaven, You are there; if I make my bed in hell, behold, You are there. If I take the wings of the morning, and dwell in the uttermost parts of the sea, even there Your hand shall lead me, and Your right hand shall hold me. If I say, 'surely the darkness shall fall on me,' even the night shall be light about me; indeed, the darkness shall not hide from You, but the night shines as the day; the darkness and the light are both alike to You." (Ps. 139:5-12)*

I am struggling to remain conscious of the word "gentle" that I used in the chapter title and still be loyal to the meaning of rationality as I have used it in this book.

Balaam, yes the jenny (donkey) beater, found it difficult to be gentle to Balak when confronted with what God put in his mouth. God was patient and did not give up on the donkey beater.

> *"God is not a man, that He should lie, nor a son of man, that He should repent. Has He said, and will He not do? Or has He spoken, and will He not make it good?" (Num. 23:19)*

If we are planning an evil deed that God promises to judge, it is not sound rationality to assume that God will repent, that is change his mind, and not punish us. The sureness of God, called in our definition of God His immutability, should allay rational fears, not increase them. God is more predictable over one thousand years than we are for one hour.

One reason to have a healthy rational fear of God is that He is bigger and stronger than us and we would lose every fight. I was the youngest of five brothers, and like all brothers, there were fights. I remember ignoring bystanders' warnings, "Dan, he is bigger than you." Often, I did not heed their wise counsel and took a beating. Fear is not the effective caution sign we hope it would be. Yes, all mortal beings are stuck in time and space, and often live immediately, not protecting their long-term welfare.

Just last week I heard that 25 million have died from AIDS, and 40 million more are infected with the HIV virus. Yes, many of these are innocent, but nowhere near this number. I do not think the passion of sex has ears to hear the warning of fear. Surely we find sex an immediate experience in marriage or otherwise. Perhaps immediacy is its tug toward waywardness.

There is something wrong with the way unbelievers assimilate the warnings of fear. At moments, I have thought that they were betting on the Fates, the three goddesses of destiny in Greek and Roman mythology. At that time, I think I saw the excitement of betting on chance. The only value chance has is a statistical value. In logical thinking, chance is nothing. It cannot offer information about Ultimate Reality. It does not even offer vector.

We are dependent beings, whether or not we are anxious about it. Attempting to break the Creator/creature equation is called rebellion in Sacred Scripture. This should elicit traumatic fear. God's response to rebellion is always the same: turn with repentance for forgiveness or persist and suffer punishment. No mortal has broken the equation, but the equation has broken many a man. Mammals that live long have well-developed neo-cellular brain areas where fear occurs. Such development can deny an invitation to a predator's dinner.

If you love life, well-reasoned fear that is moderate can help you stay alive. God is the author of life and if He be immutable, and He is, He will never turn against life as such.

CHAPTER 38
Fear, a Believer's Rationality

The long-running television series *Gunsmoke*, starring James Arness as Dodge City's Matt Dillon, had a scene where Matt was asked, "Aren't you ever afraid?" to which he responded, "The man that is not afraid is a fool." The mature Christian does not expect to live without a healthy respect for evil and a redeeming awe of God. The fear the Dodge City marshal spoke of was the lifejacket you keep on, even when you are in a lifeboat.

Believers' fear avoids polar-minded thinking about God. That is, it avoids panic and it avoids ignoring just who God is as Ultimate Reality. It most assuredly avoids despair. A devout Christian never calls a brother a fool, but a believer knows forthright that any fellow being who refuses to acknowledge that he is a creature dependent on more than himself has evolved a foolish rationality. Let's return to simple profundity. How long can you live, say, without oxygen? This is simple, because a child knows this. It is profound because no human life exists without oxygen. Put the two together and simple profundity is in evidence. To choose one without the other is polar-minded thinking.

That life is sustained or there is no life is acknowledged by all men of science. Science has not found the totally self-existent being. The believer knows One and bets his eternal soul on that very Being. The believer bows low to acknowledge that before man was created, and before a life-sustaining habitat was created, God already was from eternity. Plato reasoned to such necessary reality, simply because from nothing, nothing comes. Better English reads that from nothing, something cannot possibly come. Survivors' fear begins with knowing who God is, not from surviving an inflated self. At the most elementary level, we must know we are not self-sustaining.

The very names of God cause me to sit erect and pay attention. The word meaning of one's name in Scripture goes far beyond simply identity to core character. What is the true nature of the being? A name we all know is Jesus, which means "Jesus is the deliverer." The angel Gabriel, after assuring Mary that she should not fear, said, "You will conceive in your womb and bring forth a Son, and shall call His name Jesus" (Luke 1:31). Neither Mary nor her cousin Elizabeth had a baby-naming party. God took no chance that either John the Baptizer or Jesus would receive the wrong name. It is very difficult for any westerner to appreciate the Hebraic usage of the names for God. "O Lord, our Lord, How excellent is Your name in all the earth" (Ps. 8:1).

It serves my purpose to define only a few names for God used in the Bible that elicit awe in the believer and fear of rejection in the unbeliever. The names of God quoted are from *Systematic Theology*, by L. Berkhof.

- Él, Élohim and Élyon: point to God as the strong and mighty One, derived from the root "to be smitten with fear."
- Ádonai meaning Judge and Ruler. God is the Almighty Judge and Ruler.
- Shaddai and Él-Shaddai: Possessing all power in heaven and earth.
- Yahweh and Yaweh Tsebhaoth. In this name, God reveals Himself as the God of grace, unmerited favor toward the lesser sinner being, man. This name gradually supplanted earlier names. Israel thought this name too sacred to pronounce or spell out for fear of blasphemy.[23]

With the coming of Yahweh in the flesh, who was Jesus, the subject of panic fear was often addressed by Him with "peace be with you," or "fear not." Jesus said to His disciples:

> *"And do not fear those who kill the body but cannot kill the soul. But rather fear Him who is able to destroy both soul and body in hell." (Matt. 10:28)*

God's justice did not vanish from the cosmos with the coming of Yahweh. Yahweh, Jesus, the Christ will return as Judge. If we reject the grace of Yahweh, we will face the justice of Adonai. Redeeming love is the answer if you/we act on it.

We are to be in deep awe of God, not of others or of being "politically correct," for He alone holds ultimate power; for He alone is Ultimate Being. I wish I could grow elephant ears that I might better hear God.

God did not reveal Himself all at once and immediately (Heb. 1:1-3). The sober reality that is in place is that if you, an unbeliever, persist, you will face God in the person of the first three names I briefly described.

All who are born of woman are bastards, born outside the family of God. Believers are born again, in this life, by the power of God's Spirit, into the family of God—the same family of which Jesus is the first born, as was Adam the first born. The true believer is actually denied panic fear of God, yet he is so awed by God, he cannot help but worship God. Belief in Jesus takes us from panic fear on death row to worship in the sanctuary.

CHAPTER 39

Unbeliever, Someone's Out to Get You

There is a story early on in Genesis of two brothers, Cain and Abel:

> "Now Adam knew Eve his wife, and she conceived and bore
> Cain, and said, 'I have acquired a man from the Lord.' Then
> she bore again, this time his brother Abel. Now Abel was a
> keeper of sheep, but Cain was a tiller of the ground. And in the
> process of time it came to pass that Cain brought an offering
> of the fruit of the ground to the Lord. Abel also brought of the
> firstborn of his flock and of their fat. And the Lord respected
> Abel and his offering, but He did not respect Cain and his
> offering. And Cain was very angry, and his countenance
> fell. So the Lord said to Cain, 'Why are you angry? And why
> has your countenance fallen? If you do well, will you not be
> accepted? And if you do not do well, sin lies at the door. And its
> desire is for you, but you should rule over it.'" (Gen. 4:1-7)

There is more than one lesson in this passage. One answer is where
babies come from. In the Biblical meaning, they come following a man

knowing a woman, just in case some fast reader missed that point. My intent runs deeper than any possible humor. Even in a human plane, creature to creature, we are not the genesis of our being, any more than we are self-existing.

Psychologists are slow learners, because they only study faulted beings. In the language of psychology, God told Cain that his low self-esteem resulted from his negative performance. In contemporary psychology, someone should have gotten on Adam and Eve to bolster Cain's self-esteem. Then he would have brought the right offering, as God directed. Behavior molds character, not the other way around. Neurotic behavior makes neurotics, not the other way around. This is another reason mortals cannot separate sin from sinners, even with euphemisms.

This very evening, CBS News reported on children's soccer teams, under the direction of a developmental psychologist someplace outside Boston, that do not keep any score. The psychologist said first to develop skill for self-esteem, then later truly compete. This makes self-esteem the sacred cow. To hell with the competitive skills! Self-esteem is more a feeling than an acquired skill. I ask who then determines skill if it is not the self. This is the same kind of convoluted reasoning in the first place that got Cain messed up. The self, unless contested, always over-evaluates itself, by itself. This is the case of faulted (dumb) reasoning in egotism. If we perform well by the evaluation of God and others, self-esteem is all but a moot subject, emotionally speaking.

Cain may have come to God for counseling. It is possible. He did not follow God's advice. He did not change his behavior. He took such action that would deny anyone the opportunity of comparing him to Abel. No one compares the living with the dead. It is verse seven that releases the arrow to the heart of the human ego. The English Standard Version (1995) reads "And if you do not do well sin is crouching at the door. Its desire is for you." The Hebrew suggests a threatening demon crouching outside the door of a house. Dan, are you suggesting the demon made Cain kill his brother Abel? No, but Cain left ajar the door to his inner being, when he did not follow God's counsel. The devil was in on it because he loves death for death's sake.

Eve, "the mother of all living," was soon to have no sons. Can you enter her grief? Evil won a round. If individual self-esteem is solely the business of the individual self, why did it emotionally disembowel Cain's mother, Eve?

Unbeliever, it takes a lot out of me to warn you that if you reject God so as not to be ruled, another will rule you. I know you will hate that. It is part and parcel of being a dependent being. This is what makes it hard for me to write. Like you, I too came into existence when my father knew my mother. I am no angel on an earthly mission.

I am going with the Ruler who is the Author of Life and loves life, because the other ruler is the author of sin and loves death. You may say I have no right to say that, not even an academic right. I have as much right to say that as you have the right to say that two and two equal four. Right equates with truth. Truth and reality are the same. The fact that we are dependent and not self-existing, nor self-sustaining creatures is as much reality as two plus two equals four. Science can find no self-sustaining creatures. None of us can separate truth from reality. Who would want to? If you do, do not forget to charge the Devil rent, for he is a resident in your brain. Include a clause in your lease for property damage.

Guess who will determine your ruler? You are the man! We do not have a choice as to whether or not we will live a dependent life, but we do have a choice between good and evil, between the one True God and the Evil One.

> *"I call heaven and earth as witnesses today against you, that I have set before you life and death, blessing and cursing; therefore choose life, that both you and your descendants may live" (Deut. 30:19).*

I never would have thought of inanimate nature witnessing my wrong choices. Some of my sins I have tried to bury in the desert. Little did

I realize then that I was handing a viable witness evidence against me. Nature witnessed against Cain, for God said to Cain, "The voice of your brother's blood cries out to Me from the ground" (Gen. 4:10).

CHAPTER 40
Meet a Famous Cosmic Believer: Meet the Devil

I do not write to introduce you to a cosmic foreigner in your life's experience. You have already met him many times, whether or not you have consciously recognized him. Bluntly, I write to caution you of the real possibility of meeting him in your bathroom mirror.

When the Blessed Savior attempted to prepare His disciples for His pending sacrificial death, Peter jumped in to offer human help, humane help.

> *"Then Peter took Him aside and began to rebuke Him, saying, 'Far be it from You, Lord; this shall not happen to You!' But He turned and said to Peter, 'Get behind me, Satan! You are an offense to Me, for you are not mindful of the things of God, but the things of men.' Then Jesus said to His disciples, 'If anyone desires to come after Me, let him deny himself, and take up his cross, and follow Me. For whoever desires to save his life will lose it, but whoever loses his life for My sake will find it. For what profit is it to a man if he gains the whole world, and loses*

his own soul? Or what will a man give in exchange for his soul?"' (Matt. 16:22-26)

What Peter did wrong is self-explained by Jesus. Putting it into the vernacular of this book, Jesus said you are on the wrong end of the Creator/creature equation. In specific content, Jesus said get on your end of the Redeemer/redeemed equation. Jesus did not, by the power of His word, change Peter into the devil incarnate. Still, the Devil was in Peter when he said this, and Satan was the dominant personality for a moment.

How very human Peter's objection was and how humane was his motive. The Blessed Savior must not suffer such a cursed death. Perish the thought that the Son of God would be cursed. Those of you who believe and promulgate unconditional love should drop to your knees and ask God to let you meet the Lamb of God. I mean the kind of love that would avoid all morals and God's holiness which results in justice. The only thing "unconditional" is the offer of life and even that must be received in the context of Redeemer/sinner. You cannot receive the offer if you are still playing the devil by simply demanding a self-determined autonomous role in relation to Ultimate Reality. By rejecting God's redemption in Christ, you are so close to being your own devil that I fear to write it. This is exactly where Peter's rationality was when Jesus called him by Satan's name. I am sure Peter was paralyzed in his mind and momentarily frozen in heart. His heart missed more than one beat. In rebellion against God, you can go full circle and meet yourself. When you meet yourself, you will not like the name Jesus used. Return with me for a moment to a passage from Scripture previously quoted.

> *"I call heaven and earth as witnesses today against you, that I have set before you life and death, blessing and cursing; therefore choose life, that both you and your descendants may live; that you may love the Lord your God, that you may obey His voice, and that you may cling to Him, for He is your life and the length of your days ..." (Deut. 30:19-20a)*

In the quote above you can be a son of God and not a son of the Devil. That is your only choice, between those two. You may ask, "Do I know enough to live like a child of God? What about the many mysteries that are not yet known?" Moses, in Deuteronomy, addresses your question.

> *"The secret things belong to the Lord our God, but those things which are revealed belong to us and to our children forever, that we may do all the words of this law." (Deut. 29:29)*

Christ did not condemn Peter to hell, a place He prepared for Satan and his fallen angels. There is a quote in Acts from one of Peter's sermons and also in his second epistle where he warns of playing the role of the Devil (2 Pet. 2:4).

> *"The word which God sent to the children of Israel, preaching peace through Jesus Christ—He is Lord of all—that word you know, which was proclaimed throughout all Judea, and began from Galilee after the baptism which John preached: how God anointed Jesus of Nazareth with the Holy Spirit and with power, who went about doing good and healing all who were oppressed by the devil, for God was with Him." (Acts 10:36-38)*

It is my deliberate intent to shock the reader somewhat, as Jesus shocked Peter. But if I could blow some dust out of the fissures of your cerebral cortex, surely I would, for better, not for worse. If you are an unbeliever, you are more like the Devil in God's eyes than you are the person you perceive yourself to be. The same logic follows through for the believer in the Christian era. You are more like Christ in God's eyes than you are the self you perceive yourself to be. In God's view, there is no slight variance between believers in His Son and disbelievers. They are poles apart. Yet grace makes it easy for the unbeliever to permanently close the gap.

Christ did not come to die for us to show that He was all love. He came and died to protect us from God's wrath. God's wrath is God's enraged holiness. Love was sacrificial pouring out of Himself for sinners. Christ's love was stepping between God and us. It was receiving God's most wrathful engine. God's love dismissed nothing without the sacrificial blood of Christ. As for my personal salvation, upon accepting myself as mortal, I would judge myself insane if I did not accept forgiveness from the Ultimate Antecedent.

CHAPTER 41
Meet the Devil, a Sharper Focus

If you had to write a comprehensive paper on a subject that displeases God the most, I doubt very much if you could do better than to write on the personality of Satan and his activities in a positive mode. Should you ever set out to displease God, I pray you never impersonate or imitate the Devil. In the human arena, you might try breaking all the Ten Commandments with your very best efforts.

My chapter title promises you a closer look at Satan. Satan is not a fallen god. He is not a fallen man. Satan was created and still is an angel of God's original creation of angels. We know very little of that creation. This very powerful angel fell to pride, one of the seven deadly sins. The seven sins are deadly because they beget lesser sins. None of us needs an introduction to pride. It is just another word for egotism.

> *"How you are fallen from heaven, O Lucifer, son of the morning! How you are cut down to the ground, you who weakened the nations! For you have said in your heart: 'I will ascend into heaven, I will exalt my throne above the stars of God; I will also sit on the mount of the congregation on the farthest sides of the north; I will ascend above the heights of the clouds, I will*

> *be like the Most High.' Yet you shall be brought down to Sheol,*
> *to the lowest depths of the Pit." (Isa. 14:12-15)*

I will read no symbolism into Isaiah's writing.

We all took a great fall in Adam, but Lucifer, "Son of the morning," took a greater fall from a higher level in the order of heaven. Worst of all, nowhere in Scripture do we read of any possible redemptive life like we all are offered. Paul writes in Timothy that something analogous to what happened to Satan can happen to leaders in the church if pride is not controlled.

> *"… not a novice, lest being puffed up with pride he fall into*
> *the same condemnation as the devil. Moreover he must have*
> *a good testimony among those who are outside, lest he fall into*
> *reproach and the snare of the devil." (1 Tim. 3:7)*

I introduced St. Paul's quote to show how very much like us are the personalities of the angels, including Satan's. We can analyze Satan's personality as we would assess any other leader, whether Napoleon or Caesar. The Bible is clear that the first transgression of Satan was inordinate pride that ended up as full rebellion. He was the first to break the equation of Creator/creature, at least the first on record. He could not have been an unbeliever, because he had a warped desire to take God's place. He was no pussycat, because he took on Jesus while acknowledging right well who Jesus really was. He too is a dependent creature who has existence, and with existence he must act, and since he is evil, his actions will be evil. As to his influence on us, the Reverend A. E. Laurence of Haverhill, Massachusetts, writing at the turn of the century, said: "If God communicates with good men without their consciousness, there is no apparent reason why Satan may not, without their consciousness, communicate with bad men."[24] Satan communicates with unbelievers, not to their welfare but to cleverly manipulate them to his ends. Satan is a dedicated imitator of Christ in promoting his ends. It is difficult for me to conceive of someone who is all bad, always.

Later, Rev. Lawrence goes on to argue that good beings influence good people to be better, and evil beings influence bad men to be worse. The believer has help with his belief, as the unbeliever has help with his disbelief. I think he is saying we all are communal beings, whether we like it or not. We are also influenced by beings higher in order than ourselves. I know unbelievers who would never believe Satan has them for a target. Satan works hardest where he has the best success. The Devil never discriminates. He will accept you.

> *"And you He made alive, who were dead in trespasses and sins, in which you once walked according to the course of this world, according to the prince of the power of the air, the spirit who now works in the sons of disobedience." (Eph. 2:1-2)*

Unbelief is disbelief. Belief is not an autonomous option for man. We are commanded by God to believe. We are all born sons of disobedience.

I am afraid for people when I hear them boast that they will take Satan down. His strength commands respect from unbelievers and believers alike. Angels are of a higher "species."

There is a very short Epistle of Jude just before the last book in the Bible that speaks to proper respect for Satan:

> *"And the angels who did not keep their proper domain, but left their own abode, He has reserved in everlasting chains under darkness for the judgment of the great day; as Sodom and Gomorrah, and the cities around them in a similar manner to these, having given themselves over to sexual immorality and gone after strange flesh, are set forth as an example, suffering the vengeance of eternal fire. Likewise also these dreamers defile the flesh, reject authority, and speak evil of dignitaries. Yet Michael the archangel, in contending with the devil, when*

he disputed about the body of Moses, dared not bring against him a reviling accusation but said, 'The Lord rebuke you!' But these speak evil of whatever they do not know; and whatever they know naturally, like brute beasts, in these things they corrupt themselves." (Jude 1:6-10)

For those of you who slept in Sunday School, Michael was one of the chief angels who won the war in heaven with Lucifer and his followers. No mere man really wants to take Satan on, even though his sentence has already been pronounced. Satan has nothing to lose.

I remember working with a murderer sentenced to die. I also remember his words to me. "Dan, I like you, but I have nothing to lose, so guard yourself." Was I frightened? You bet your psyche I was. No, he did not escape. No, I did not kill him. Satan has absolutely nothing to lose, so will you be careful? Will you seek help from the One who can handle him?

"And war broke out in heaven: Michael and his angels fought with the dragon; and the dragon and his angels fought, but they did not prevail, nor was a place found for them in heaven any longer. So the great dragon was cast out, that serpent of old, called the Devil and Satan, who deceives the whole world; he was cast to the earth, and his angels were cast out with him. Then I heard a loud voice saying in heaven, 'Now salvation, and strength, and the kingdom of our God, and the power of His Christ have come, for the accuser of our brethren, who accused them before our God day and night, has been cast down. And they overcame him by the blood of the Lamb and by the word of their testimony, and they did not love their lives to the death. Therefore rejoice, O heavens, and you who dwell in them! Woe to the inhabitants of the earth and the sea! For the devil has come down to you, having great wrath because he knows that he has a short time." (Rev. 12:7-12)

Unbeliever, Satan is not your friend. He wants you dead and he wants me dead. He has a taste and passion for death. His passion for evil is insatiable. If you take him on or sell your soul to him, he will flatten you like a corn tortilla. God is high bidder on your soul. It is a historical fact that he will pay a Divine price for it.

CHAPTER 42
A Very Personal Demon

Our very personal demon is egoism. In some of us, it is the more degenerative egotism. This chapter is composed of excerpts of an article I wrote this past April to hospital chaplains, entitled *Will You Survive Altruism?* Be we atheists, theists, murderers, saints, et cetera, we all carry the seeds of egoism in our soul. The seed sower is the demon at Cain's door.

In 1850, Auguste Comte coined the word *altruism* to contrast egoism. Few of us would need help with the word *egoism*. It is valuing everything only in reference to one's personal interest. There is no need to coin any new words to understand egoism. *Webster's Third New International Dictionary* gives us about 482 words where *self* is the prefix, as in self-esteem, self-evaluation, et cetera. Altruism, still a noun, is uncalculated in consideration of devotion to others. The same dictionary refers to altruism as an extreme Christian virtue contrasting egoism. For me, Christian altruism is calculated consideration and the very conscious realization that there will be sacrifice and there will be loss. Other worldly rewards are not assessable psycho-sociologically because they are without the scope of this inquiry. Such immediate "heavenly" consciousness misses the mark of uniquely Christian altruism in pastoral care. They belong in our prayers and meditation, not to mention God's covenant promises.

When I am in a "training" session for chaplaincy, I can only think that by all that is analogous, we should have flunked Logic 201. There we were taught that in order to have realized being, there must be Ultimate Being, and in order to realize virtue, as in altruism, there must be absolute Altruism. Christ was the only absolute Altruist known to the world. We have fallen into the pit of secularism when it comes to reliable definitions. There are no solely human criteria for evaluation of being or virtue, nor can there be.

The ethic that says everyone's value is equal and that everyone's values must be honored and accepted equally is secular relativism, drifting toward nihilism. The insanity of such a philosophy is that it is enforced by the very rule it denies as having any reality. Different self values not related to Ultimate Value (God) simply cannot share equal value. Each creature has being value to God, but even that criterion takes us out of relativism, atheism, and secularism, into theism. Secularism dances to the music of public opinion or polls. Does anyone consider that if everyone on earth were an egotistical being, the value of all would not increase from the value of one egotistical being? Surely the harm would increase. Community would then be non-existent. Any faith in God would be momentary and vaporous. Egoism and faith in God are no more analogous than egoism and altruism are analogous.

Equality before God is a common denominator, not an individualistic one. Sadly, an egotistical numerator cannot count to two.

Theism stands out in altruism; atheism is egoism. In no other world religion, past or present, did Deity come to rescue man in unqualified altruism. Do we truly grasp this? Christ is identified with His people in a union so intimate that whatever happens to Him happens to them. All His acts are the acts, not of a private, but of a public person. "In Christ all shall be made alive" (1 Cor. 15:22). We all know what He laid aside in heaven. Secular ism says love yourself so you may then love others. Is this true? Self-approval stands above self-love when it measures itself by the blessed Savior. Egoism measures itself by itself. St. Paul in 2 Cor. 10:12 is right on point.

The more we study altruism in biology, the more we diminish its cogent virtue. Christ, the Holy One, invaded nature, especially the realm of man's nature. In history, we killed Him because He said He was of, and was, Divine Being, not natural being. In some contemporary hospitals, we post bold signs "DO NOT RESUSCITATE." We have driven a steel wedge between Christian altruism and the patients because we refuse to recognize the reality that the Kingdom of God is not solely realized by natural sight (Matt. 25:44-46). You cannot have Christian sacrifice if *Christian* is indefinable. I have tried to define it by tying us with a tight tether to the equation of Redeemer/redeemed. It is a very private demon because Satan will mold that lesser demon to defeat our very unique and individualistic personality. As God told Cain, "You must control it."

Egotism is the demon fuel that powers more flights to hell than any other energy source.

CHAPTER 43
Analysis of Disbelief

"Without the radical gift of God's transforming love in grace, we are lost, helpless, rebellious, and defensively self-grounded, and we constitute the most lethal element in the universe. Faith is the response to grace in and by which we are transformed and restored." James W. Fowler, Dictionary of Pastoral Care on Counseling.[25]

The most important word for my chapter title in Dr. Fowler's quote is "self-grounded." Self-grounding is the second half of the Creator/creature equation that I keep referring to throughout the book. Half is not an adequate concept to express the reality, since both parties to the equation are not self-existent and both parties are not self-dependent. Self-grounding is not relational at all. As I stated earlier, belief is commanded in Scripture and is not just an option in the cafeteria of many world views. Why center self in a mortal creature, cursed by sin, that is going to die? To choose self is to guarantee you lose, if not today, then in three score and seven.

What most unbelievers refuse to acknowledge is that to choose self is to reject relationships. To choose self-centeredness is also to reject transcendent meaning. To choose self-centeredness is to deny any obedience, even to our natural habitat on which we are dependent for life itself. To push self-centeredness to its maximum extreme is to attend your own funeral by yourself. Who is going to throw the dirt over you? You should pre-arrange care of your dead body.

Earlier, I wrote that Adam knew Eve and Cain was born. Logic says that one and one are two, yet when we have a one-and-one relationship with the Biblical verb "know," we have one and one equaling three. Relationships are costly to surrender.

Self-centeredness evolved the necessity of the billion-plus self-help books. Research now shows that many an author made a lot of money without any benefit to the reader that can be shown. Whenever we break the Creator/creature equation, every purposed theory has a shorter lifespan than mortal man does himself. I have been told by unbelievers that while they reject God, they accept nature, that is the earth, for the earth is also eternal. First and foremost, the earth is not eternal, for nature changes, and what changes cannot, by its essence, be eternal. Alister McGrath of Oxford University puts us in our place if we would bet that nature would take care of us eternally. Besides, we are the stewards of nature, not the reverse.

> *"If anything can be identified as the enemy of those who care for creation, it is the ruthless human tendency to exploit and refuse to accept that limits have been set for human behavior and activity, either by nature itself or by God. The fundamental element of Original Sin (as described in Genesis 3) is a desire to 'be like God' and to be set free from all the restraints of creatureliness. This resolute refusal to accept a properly constituted place within creation can easily be seen to be linked with the development of tools by which humanity is no longer obligated to operate under any form of moral or physical restraint." The Reenactment of Nature.*[26]

Self-centeredness denies the care of the earth rather than guarantees it. Self-grounding is playing with a god vis-à-vis the image in your bathroom mirror. I am quite aware that I veered off specific subject course, but such is the nature of disbelief. It is truly the natural course of disbelief. Disbelief turns out to be almost never based on serious study, which makes it an excuse, not a studied conviction in one's disbelief. Were you able to follow me?

I refuse to go A to Z through the excuses for disbelief, because my imagination, in this area as a believer in God, is limited. The unbeliever's mind can take flight every which way when it is self-grounded because the imagination of the self must protect the previous commitment to self-imaging.

Excuses lack the cogent spice of reason to be true—to be accepted. As I stated early in the book, rationality is a matter of how one believes, not what one believes. The integrity of personality gets connected to self-grounding, not to beliefs. The view of disbelief is never quite worth fighting for, but personal integrity is worth dying for.

I once befriended a two-time killer who was acquitted on the trial of his first murder. He shared his self-grounding reality of that murder with me. Following the second murder, I asked him why! Why? He told me that both murders were his, and the judicial system wrenched the first from him. He killed the second time to protect his personal integrity as a murderer. Yes, Dr. Fowler, we are lethal.

Once upon a time in Tucson, Arizona, while treating an offender who completely lost identity in nihilism, I took him out of jail and into the desert. There I had him dig a substantial hole and carefully autograph it. There was no dialogue, just my instructions. One week later, I took him back out in the desert. He responded, "That is my hole, look!" I would not dream of asking him to cover it. Later, of course, it did fill in.

The two stories simply show the connectedness of personality and beliefs held. The first man was morally quite wrong. The second had to begin life over as a child and connected belief to evidentiary experience.

In my analysis of unbelief, I think I have shown that it is determined by more than a cogent agency in the head of a man from truth available to him for consideration. The rational mind does not always survive the drive of the self for self-grounding independent of Ultimate Reality, that is God.

Both believers and unbelievers display great trust, but they differ in whom it is grounded. The unbeliever is chained to selectivity of evidence to protect self-grounding. His fear factor is extant, that is it is existing and known. Only the being holding a Judeo-Christian view can function with the shutters to his mind always opened and never threatened by mere evidence alone.

CHAPTER 44
Philosophy Speaks Up For God

Earlier in the book, I expressed my negative feeling about writing an apologetic defense for the existence of God. My philosophy is based largely on the fact that it is not found in Sacred Scripture with much emphasis. Genesis begins with God's Eternal Being extant, existent, and known. Belief requires my acceptance of God's introductory sentence, and nothing in philosophy or science seriously disputes it. When we get to the book of Romans in the New Testament, again not only are we required to know and acknowledge God's Eternal Being, but also His invisible attributes. When you know someone's attributes, you have a genuine acquaintance with them. You could attest to their genuine character.

Note that Paul, while writing under the inspiration of the Holy Spirit, does not state existence. If we have attributes we must acknowledge Being:

> *"For the wrath of God is revealed from heaven against all*
> *ungodliness and unrighteousness of men, who suppress the*
> *truth in unrighteousness, because what may be known of God*
> *is manifest in them, for God has shown it to them. For since*
> *the creation of the world His invisible attributes are clearly*
> *seen, being understood by the things that are made, even His*

eternal power and Godhead, so that they are without excuse."
(Rom. 1:18-20)

Aristotle believed that all humans, by nature, wanted to know. Philosophy is simply a love of wisdom. It is a tool for thinking clearly about faith and seeing the implications for living. I believe that is what St. Paul is saying to the Romans. From creation of the cosmos, you should have reasoned to some conclusions. The story is told at the Lear Jet Corporation that $14,000 was allocated to study the amount of head padding to put in the cockpit. (In the late fifties, that was money.) When it was completed, they called Wilber Lear, who got in the cockpit, banged his head against the padding, and said, "Use more padding."

In this age of phenomenology, a world of sense experience, just move your body at walking pace into a tree and I promise you, you will be conscious of created nature, not to mention being. Nothing comes from nothing and from nothing, nothing can come. Something must have always been transcendent of nature. Something must have been in existence before nature, before the cosmos was brought into existence. Material cannot start from nothing and bring itself into existence. It did not come from nothing, because only nothing can proceed from nothing. Even nothing cannot have motion from nothing.

If you cannot grasp this during a five-minute pause to reason and exercise your God-given rationality, I beg of you with sincerity and pathos quicken your steps and try the tree experience again. Surely I would prefer that you sit at poolside with a member of the opposite sex and a cold drink of lemonade and experience the reality of your having worthwhile and attractive being. At one time in his life, Socrates said, "I don't know anything, but at least I know that I don't know anything." Surely he was exaggerating his humility, for he came to believe many profound things. Even in humility, Socrates strongly affirmed the reality of his being. Both Socrates and especially Plato reasoned to transcendent being and came close to declaring Eternal Being.

If you find yourself unable to reason from yourself to some transcendent being, you have an ego problem capable of doing you in, even to your self-demise. I am not talking down to you, the reader; I am talking you up to your potential of a being created in the image and likeness of God.

Dr. R. C. Sproul, who appears as comfortable with philosophy as he is with theology, writes in *Reason to Believe:* "If something exists now, we must affirm one of three things about it. It is either eternal, created by something that is eternal, or self-created."[27] He challenges us to come up with alternatives that adhere to sound logic. One and two establish an eternal Creator. He goes on to state that most unbelievers opt for number three. Here the mind can take flight without filing a flight plan with the tower of reason. If you choose self-created, you go into "Star Wars Science" and bring down your spacecraft with just two sentences.

> *"Obviously, for something to create itself, it would have to exist in order to create. It would have to exist before it existed if it were to create its own existence ... For something to create itself, it would have to be and not be at the same time and have the same relationship."*[28]

Having taught basic logic and philosophy, I am sensitive to the fact that it is difficult for some students. If you think God is just cuddly teddy-bear love and would never require us to flog our minds, listen to how He addressed Job after allowing Satan to walk Job through hell on earth.

> *"Then the Lord answered Job out of the whirlwind, and said: 'Who is this who darkens counsel by words without knowledge? Now prepare yourself like a man; I will question you, and you shall answer me. Where were you when I laid the foundations of the earth? Tell Me, if you have understanding. Who determined its measurements? Surely you know!'" (Job 38:1–5)*

When it comes to answering God, being a dependent being stuck in time and space is a frightening negative handicap. Life is easier when we start with "In the beginning God." Your brain will hurt less. A word to the true believer: If you feel I give too much credit to Plato, Socrates, and other philosophers for their interest in the ultimate, may I remind you that they lived before God's self-revelation in Christ (Heb. 1:1-6). They also preceded the coming of the Holy Spirit (Acts 2:1-21).

CHAPTER 45

What Are You Doing About Your Sins?

Diogenes (412?-233 BC) was a Greek philosopher who is said to have walked around in the daytime light, carrying a lighted lantern. When asked the reason for this, he would say, "I am searching for an honest man." Had Diogenes asked another, "Have you ever sinned?" he could have blown out his lantern. The vast, vast majority of us would admit to sin, yet the vast number have not dealt with the problem.

The prosaic, matter-of-fact problem that Scripture presents to us is, if we do not deal with the problem, God surely will. Had Diogenes been looking for a totally honest man, he could have blown his lantern out upon meeting Jesus, because He was One of a kind.

I am sure you heard that God is love. He always was and still is. Yet God's most distinctive characteristic is His holiness. Surely it is realized if you compare God to man. He is also unlimited justice. We have a historical record of Jesus's definition of love, "Greater love has no man than this, than to lay down one's life for his friends" (John 15:13). It is documented, historical fact that He met the standard He set. From His own words, we read:

"Therefore My Father loves Me, because I lay down My life that I may take it again. No one takes it from Me, but I lay it down of Myself. I have power to lay it down, and I have power to take it again. This command I have received from My Father." (John 10:17-18)

God's love is not unconditional because love can be rejected. True love is Divine, sacrificial Love. The concept of unconditional love was authored and nurtured in secularism so as to be in harmony with amoral values. Unconditional love would compromise God's holiness and justice which cannot ever be negotiated. If you believe that Jesus died a sacrificial death for you God will credit you if you receive it based on acknowledged need. For me, I carry with me an acknowledged, conscious, on-going need of Divine help. My ego would like to shed that burden every day, ceremoniously.

Should you ask if it was not the Roman soldiers that killed Christ, you would be accurate. Scriptural truths often appear as dualism. The Creator/creature equation offers many such possibilities. That God's holiness cannot absorb sin is also verified from the lips of Christ. Matthew records His words:

"And about the ninth hour Jesus cried out with a loud voice, saying, 'Eli, Eli, lama sabachthani?' that is, 'My God, My God, why have You forsaken Me?'" (Matt. 27:46)

The Apostle Paul explained the meaning of all this in God's sight. "For He made Him, who knew no sin to be sin for us, that we might become the righteousness of God in Him," (2 Cor. 5:21) No mere mortal could ever discover such love. No mere mortal would have ever dreamed it. None of the gods of the many religions of the world even suggest it. Some suggest you sacrifice to them. The most selfish and dependent human on earth would have never dared to ask for it. He would have been too self-grounded to think of it.

If all the above is historical truth, what must we do to be saved? There is a story from history that quickly gets to the point. Paul and Silas were imprisoned for telling the story I told above and saying that this was the true and only way to God. They also taught that God and Christ are one and the same God.

> "Suddenly there was a great earthquake, so that the foundations of the prison were shaken; and immediately all the doors were opened and everyone's chains were loosed. And the keeper on the prison, awaking from sleep and seeing the prison doors open, supposing the prisoners had fled, drew his sword and was about to kill himself. But Paul called with a loud voice, saying, 'Do yourself no harm, for we are all here.' Then he called for a light, ran in, and fell down trembling before Paul and Silas. And he brought them out and said, 'Sirs, what must I do to be saved?' So they said, 'Believe on the Lord Jesus Christ, and you will be saved, you and your household.' Then they spoke the word of the Lord to him and to all who were in his house." (Acts 16:26–32)

What is the meaning of the message of the Lord Paul taught in the language I have been using in this book? If you have placed your confidence in your own self-grounding, you must break that cement with a heavy sledgehammer and acknowledge your need of Christ's help with God. Returning to the beginning of this chapter, you must deal with the sin problem most men acknowledge having, and you must accept God's help, God's way. God's way is the only way to salvation from sin.

Are you good enough morally? Yes and no. If you accept help, the answer is yes, that is, good enough for God's acceptance. If you want to shop your goodness, the answer is a monster-sized "no." Upon accepting Christ's offer, you will be standing in Jesus's righteousness before God. The rest of us will experience you as very human. To believe means "to entrust or commit oneself to God's plan, not yours." Would you consider, I pray, accepting from me that that is truly a smart move? It's an intelligent move because Jesus was killed and God raised Him up from real death. You will die, hopefully not be killed, and God promises to raise you if you trust solely in Christ. This is what I did about my sins, which were so very many.

I did not clear up all the mysteries. I cannot. Yet, as we sometimes find in a court of law, "the preponderance of evidence" is for Christ.

> *"The secret things belong to the Lord our God, but those things which are revealed belong to us and to our children forever, that we may do all the words of his law." (Deut. 29:29)*

It is easy to see that the Creator/creature equation was in place when Moses wrote. It is in place now and it will forever be, whether or not we are in heaven, where Jesus will allow us to call Him our brother, or whether we are in eternal alienation in hell. If you make a full stop at the stop signs of life, you will sense His invitation:

> *"And the Spirit and the bride say, 'Come!' and let him who hears say, 'Come!' and let him who thirsts come. Whoever desires, let him take the water of life freely" (Rev. 22:17).*

How long do you have to decide? I can only say right now there is no guarantee you will be able to shelve this book or discard it. God told King Solomon he chose well when he asked for wisdom (1 Kings 3:11). How long we individually have to decide and where we will be, only God knows. God does not treat us the same when viewed from our perspective on earth. He does treat us all with Divine mercy and miraculously effective grace.

BIBLIOGRAPHIC ENDNOTES

1   Lawrence O. Richards, *Expository Dictionary of Bible Words*, (Grand Rapids, Michigan: The Zondervan Corporation, 1985), p. 252.

2   Simon Blackburn, *The Oxford Dictionary of Philosophy*, second edition, (Great Britain, Clays Ltd. 2005), p. 235.

3   C.S. Lewis, *The Case for Christianity*, (New York, Macmillan Publishing Company, 1989), p. 36.

4   John Blanchard, *Does God Believe in Atheists?* (Great Britain, Creative Point & Design – Wales, 2000) p. 21.

5   Samuel Rapport and Helen Wright, *Science: Method and Meaning*, (New York, Washington Square Pres, 1968), pp 64-86.

6   ibid. p. 21.

7   Francis A. Schaeffer, *Escape from Reason*, (Downers Grove, Illinois, Intervarsity Press, 1968), p. 83.

8   ibid., p. 123

9   Henry Campbell Black, *Black's Law Dictionary*, (St. Paul, Minn., West Publishing Co., 1968), p. 872.

10   ibid.

11   David Inglesby, "Ideology and the Human Sciences," *The Human Context*, Vol. II, No. 2, London N.W. 3, England (July 1970), p. 166.

12   Hans J. Eysenck, "The Effects of Psychotherapy," *International Journal of Psychiatry*, Vol. 1, No. 1 (Boston, Mass., The International Press, W.C.) pp. 99-138.

13   ibid, p. 176.

14   ibid, p. 15.

15   Noah Webster, *American Dictionary of the English Language*,

"Founding Father of Scholarship and Education," (San Francisco: Foundation for American Christian Education, 2000), p. 15.

[16] C.S. Lewis, *Surprised by Joy*, (London, A Harvest/HBJ Book, 1956), pp. 228-229.

[17] Kelly James Clark, Richard Lints, James K.A. Smith, *101 Key Terms in Philosophy and Their Importance to Theology*, (Louisville, Ky., John Knox Press, 2004), p. 96.

[18] ibid.

[19] E.V. Stein, *Dictionary of Pastoral Care and Counseling*, Nashville, Tenn., Abvingdon Press, 2002), p. 488.

[20] William D. Phillips, "Finding the Meaning of Human Existence," *Science and Theology News*, Vol. 10, June 2006, (Brentwood, Tn.), p. 14.

[21] ibid.

[22] ibid., p. 431.

[23] L. Berkhof, *Systematic Theology*, (Grand Rapids, Mich., Wm. D. Eerdman's Publishing Co., 1977), pp. 48-49.

[24] A. E. Laurence, *Satan, Bible Encyclopaedia and Scriptural Dictionary*, (Chicago, Ill., The Harvard-Severance Company, 1906), p. 1530.

[25] James W. Fowler, *Faith Dictionary of Pastoral Care and Counseling*, (Nashville, Tenn, Abvingdon Press, 2005), p. 396.

[26] Alister McGrath, *The Reenchantment of Nature*, (London: Doubleday/Galilee, 1003), p. 79.

[27] R. C. Sproul, *Reason to Believe* (Grand Rapids, Mich., Zondervan, 1982), p. 106.

[28] ibid.

ABOUT THE AUTHOR

The author brings twofold extensive experience to his desk for the writing of this book that balances the best of criminal justice and pastoral care. Ordained 52 years ago today he was never an organizational man. His passion for effective professional services to needy souls often nettled some officials until their own son, daughter or close friend was in trouble. Then, at times, miracles were requested. In the crime enterprise he chose criminal psychopathy and taught the subject in the Graduate School at the University of Arizona. "If you can just stay alive with those guys and girls you will be smarter tomorrow" he has been heard to say.

Sigmund Freud's niece, Dr. Melitta Schmideberg, M.D. of London, England, invited the author to write for the "International Journal of Offender Therapy and Comparative Criminology," an honor never offered to anyone else without a doctoral degree. He opposed the melting integration of Psychology and Theology because he believes the end product was predictable *a priori* given man's universal nature. He did crime scene profiling before the name became popular. The author also testified as an expert witness in cases involving criminal insanity.

The author loves man and he loves the church. His life of faith is literally readable in three books of 100 short subjects, each called words, in dialogue with the Trinity. In reviewing one of these books Jewish author, Ursula Erika Yunger, born in Berlin under Hitler's chancellorship wrote, "If I were allowed an expression to describe the effect of reading this true masterpiece of inspiration, I choose to say transcendent."

Dan's father was a Rumanian immigrant vegetable farmer. He was nurtured by the undaunted faith and prayers of his loving mother. Beginning at age 25, without one day of high school, he earned three degrees and taught eighteen different subjects while working full time with the Superior Court of Arizona. This book is his fifth. The first was adopted by the Federal Bureau of Prisons, Women's Division, as a training test. He lives in Tucson, Arizona with the lovely Melanie Lee, his wife of 36 years. The family has three sons and seven grandchildren.

Dan's mornings begin with a prayer from a collection of Puritan prayers entitled *The Valley of Vision*. He pleads, "I am a gladiator in the sands of life, not an academic spectator in the stands." Some of his readers may say what Saint Peter wrote of Saint Paul's writings: "He speaks of truths that are at times hard to understand." (2 Peter 3:16). Dan fears God because he has not been able to make a clear enough distinction between the worst sinner and holiest saint he has met. If you wish to find him, look among sinners and the needy.

Printed in the United States
106240LV00002B/1-99/P